ENGLISH ETIQUETTE

FOR

INDIAN GENTLEMEN

ENGLISH ETIQUETTE

FOR

INDIAN GENTLEMEN.

BY

W. T. WEBB, M.A.

GYAN

Published by

Gyan Publishing House
5, Ansari Road
Daryaganj, New Delhi-110002
Phone: 011-47034999, 9811692060
E-mail: books@gyanbooks.com

Distribution Network
gyanbooks.com
India, USA, Canada, UK, Australia

ISBN: 978-93-6208-630-3 (HB)
First Published, 1888

2nd Impression 2024

Printed at: Gyan Press, Delhi.

ENGLISH ETIQUETTE FOR INDIAN GENTLEMEN
Author: W.T. WEBB

ENGLISH ETIQUETTE

FOR

INDIAN GENTLEMEN.

ENGLISH ETIQUETTE

FOR

INDIAN GENTLEMEN.

BY

W. T. WEBB, M.A.,

Bengal Education Service, Author of "Indian Lyrics," "Martial for English Readers," &c.

" Manners must adorn knowledge."— CHESTERFIELD.

PREFACE.

AT a time like the present when Indian and European gentlemen and ladies are beginning to mix more freely in each other's society, it has seemed to the writer that there is a want of some kind of manual of English manners and usages, to which Indian gentlemen might refer in case of uncertainty. It is with the object of aiding and furthering in this way such friendly intercourse that the present work has been undertaken.

It will be observed that the author has endeavoured to include everything on the subject of etiquette that may be useful to *all classes* of Indian gentlemen that are or may be brought into contact with Europeans; and that, consequently, various details have been introduced, which would have been unnecessary in a book intended only for the higher and more educated classes.

The writer's best thanks are due to the Bengal Secretariat, to the Assistant Private Secretary to the Viceroy, and to the Private Secretary to the Lieutenant-Governor of Bengal for valuable help and information, as well as to several friends who have kindly looked through the proofs of this work and made sundry useful suggestions.

CONTENTS.

INTRODUCTION.

ETIQUETTE may be defined as a body of rules to guide our behaviour in polite society.

Society (by which is meant the whole community of gentlefolk in any country) has, by a general consensus of opinion, laid down these rules for its own well-being and preservation, and they are, therefore, important to all those who wish to belong to it.

To the Indian gentleman, particularly, who desires to mix in English society, a knowledge of the rules of English etiquette is important, because in its details the etiquette of one community often differs widely from that of another; and it is quite possible that tastes and habits that are approved in Indian, may be discountenanced in European, society.

To a large extent, however, these rules of conduct are the same among ladies and gentlemen everywhere, since the essence of politeness is a delicate regard for the feelings of others, and the first element of good manners is unselfishness. Thus manners are really based upon morals; and courtesy, when we come to analyse it, is found to be the outcome of the virtues of reverence, forbearance, and self-control.

For India, an era of change has begun: gradually her time-honoured customs are being modified, and her ancient landmarks removed. And there is danger that, with much that is not worth preserving, the simple dignity and refined courtesy that marked the "fine old Indian gentleman" may be thrust aside by the new ideas and levelling theories which the first superficial contact with Western knowledge and civilization brings in its train. "Let us," then, in the words of Mr. Gladstone[1] (words which young India would do well to take to heart) "remember that in our best achievements lie hid the seeds of danger; and beware lest the dethronement of Custom, to make place for Right, should displace, along with it, that principle of Reverence which bestows a discipline absolutely invaluable in the formation of character."

---

[1] *The Nineteenth Century*, Jan., 1887

CHAPTER I.

GENERAL RULES OF BEHAVIOUR, DRESS, &c.

1. To chew anything (such as *pan* or *betel*) in English society is not considered polite. Learn, therefore, to abstain from the practice when you are in the company of European gentlemen and ladies; and avoid, as far as possible, coming into their neighbourhood just after chewing without having previously cleansed your mouth. Courtesy in this matter is imperative on all Indian gentlemen who wish to show a polite consideration towards their European friends and acquaintances; just as a European gentleman would be bound not to smoke a cigar in Indian society, if he knew that it objected to the practice.

2. Do not (if you can help it) expectorate or clear your throat with a loud noise in public. If either action is necessary, retire to some private place for the purpose. In the society of English gentlemen and ladies especially the practice should be avoided. And since the sound of it is quite as unpleasant to them as the action itself, endeavour to go out of hearing whenever you indulge in it.

Again, an Indian gentleman should be careful in company to suppress "those ebullitions which are considered amongst his own people to be indicative of his having enjoyed his breakfast."[1] Hiccuping, &c., if

---

[1] *Social Life in India.*

tolerable in the home circle, is very unbecoming in public.

Try also to avoid loud coughing, or violent blowing of the nose (which should *never* be done with the fingers), &c., in public, and do not sniff or snuffle. All such noises are unpleasant to others, and therefore impolite. Lastly, when you mix in European society, never be unprovided with a pocket-handkerchief.

3. Shun the common practice, when seated, of jogging up and down with your body, or of crossing your legs, and then swinging one of them to and fro. Do not get into the way of patting or stroking any part of your person. Wherever you are, it is well to avoid these practices, because they easily grow into habits, and you will be liable to fall into them unconsciously to the annoyance of others. For the same reason, it is well to avoid the habit of lolling or lounging in your seat, or of nursing your leg. Do not stretch out your legs in front of you or spread them wide apart; and do not sit, in public, with your legs aloft upon a chair or table. Be easy, but at the same time graceful in your demeanour in public. Walk with the body erect, but not stiff: do not slouch. Let the arms swing slightly with the motion of the body. The chest should be expanded, the shoulders thrown back, and the toes only slightly turned out.

4. When you are in society, remember that it is impolite to whisper, hum, or whistle, or to break out into loud roars of laughter. Laugh, if you will, but do so gently and naturally. When laughing, do not cover your mouth with your hand. Do not drum with your fingers or twiddle your thumbs. Do not yawn, or, if you must,

place your hand before your mouth during the process. Never bite or pick your nails or scratch yourself, and avoid the little nervous gestures in which some people indulge, such as fingering their noses, or laying hold of their ears during conversation. Avoid making your toilet in public, as cleaning your nails or picking your teeth; and do not scratch your head, or pick your nose or your ear. Do not read a newspaper or a book in an audible whisper, as it disturbs those near you.

5. Avoid the use of slang expressions of any kind, either in speech or writing. It is well to eschew fine language as much as possible; but it is much more desirable to eschew slang. In the first place, since you are unfamiliar with its use, you will probably employ it incorrectly; and, in the second place, even if you do not make mistakes in using it, slang in the mouth of a foreigner sounds inappropriate. Worse than slang are English oaths, occasionally indulged in by Indian language men who wish to appear at their ease with Europeans, and who may fall into the use of bad language in society, in ignorance of the meaning or force of the words they employ. In general society, swearing, &c., whoever practises it, is always a breach of politeness.

6. An Indian gentleman, when talking to Englishmen or in their hearing, should not speak of other Englishmen, whether official or non-official, without giving them their appropriate titles. Thus, he should not say "*Brown* told me so-and-so," but *Mr. Brown*, or *Sir Richard Brown*, or *Lord Brown*, as the case may be. Also, never use the initial of a person's name to designate him or her, as *Mr. P.*, *Mrs. C.*, *Miss W.*

7. The higher classes of English people practise a greater reticence, both in speech and writing, than is customary among Indian gentlemen of the same classes; and there are several words and expressions denoting parts or functions of the human body, which are tabooed in polite society, since they suggest unpleasant ideas.

An English gentleman would not, for instance, talk about "a pain in his *stomach*," or use the word *stomach*[1] at all (in reference to himself or his friends) in ordinary conversation or correspondence, unless he were communicating with his doctor. Especially would he avoid such words in the hearing of ladies.

Should you, therefore, have occasion to ask (whether verbally or in writing) for leave on the ground of illness, do not enumerate all the particulars of your complaint; it is sufficient to state briefly what it is. Similarly, if you should compose a brief memoir or account of a friend's illness and death for the general public, do not insert unpleasant details of his disorder. You are not writing a medical diagnosis or report of his case; such frankness of expression is, therefore, unnecessary. Similarly, do not discuss ailments of any kind in company, especially when a lady is the subject of them. The mention even of some disorders (such as Diarrhœa or Dysentery) should be avoided.

There are other words and subjects, such as *adultery*, *fornication*, *childbirth*, *miscarriage*, *&c.*, of which mention should not be made in the general intercourse of polite society. In social conversation, especially when ladies

[1] "Belly" is worse still. If necessity arises, use "abdomen."

are present, it is well to avoid topics (as, for instance, Sanitation) which may lead to the introduction of words or expressions such as may offend the ears of the company.

There is, no doubt, such a thing as a too great squeamishness in matters of this kind; but it is better for an Indian gentleman mixing in European society to err on the side of over-caution than on the side of laxity regarding them.

8. In any place of public resort, such as the corridor of a public hall, or at a Garden Party or other gathering, do not stand about with your friends in knots and stare at ladies and gentlemen as they pass; or make remarks to your companions about them in their hearing. Those who are so treated will probably take no outward notice of such conduct, but they none the less recognise it as impolite towards themselves.

If you are standing in the way of any one who wants to pass you, politely make way for him at once. Avoid doing so grudgingly or as if your aim were to give him just room enough and no more. Do not be afraid that you are, under any circumstances, doing anything undignified or servile in readily drawing aside and making room for others; such conduct is one of the characteristics of the true gentleman. If any one is standing in your way, do not push past him, but say "Will you allow me to pass?" or "Excuse me."

9. Do not be over-sensitive. Learn to tolerate criticism. He that can bear to be told of his faults will the sooner learn to mend them. Do not be ready to put a bad construction upon anything that is said to or

about you, and do not take offence where none is intended. It sometimes happens that Indian gentlemen consider themselves to have been ill-treated by Europeans, simply through their misunderstanding or misconstruing words or actions of the latter. Englishmen, again, are apt, on occasion, to be somewhat rough and ready in what they say and do; but remember that such downright conduct is not necessarily overbearing, and do not convert a hasty word or what is intended only for a jest into a deadly insult. Learn, in short, to adopt a friendly attitude towards Europeans rather than one of reserve and suspicion.

10. Do not be too ready to indulge your curiosity. Thus, it is very impolite to make any attempt to look over the shoulder of any one who is reading or writing anything, as a book or a letter, without his permission. Beware of prying into matters that do not concern you. If, for example, a gentleman brings a book into the room where you are, do not try to spy out its title, much less take it up in your hands and look at it unasked. Or if, again, there is anything unusual about his dress, &c., do not stare at or draw the attention of others to the peculiarity. Never take liberties with any but your intimate friends and companions, and never intrude. People may say nothing; but they mentally resent such treatment all the same. These may perhaps seem small matters; but remember that a calm reserve of demeanour is a special mark of politeness.

11. Avoid writing begging letters, or applying for assistance to others unless you have ***solid grounds*** for believing that you have some special claim upon their

good offices, or that they are really interested in your welfare. Do not assume that a kind of universal benevolence is a quality inherent in all English gentlemen, and ask them to give you help, pecuniary or otherwise, both in season and out of season. Cultivate a habit and a feeling of independence, and learn to rely upon your own exertions rather than upon the kindness or forbearance of others for success in life.

Do not, therefore, write a letter to a stranger, begging him to defray the expenses of your education, or to a newspaper manager, asking him to supply you with his paper *gratis*, or to an author, requesting him to make you a present of his book. Be chary of appeals *ad misericordiam* (*i.e.*, to the pity of the person addressed); claims or entreaties for assistance should be based on your own merits and abilities rather than upon your poverty or misfortunes. Hence, applications for a Government or other post simply or mainly on the ground that you have a large family to support, or appeals to an examiner to give you passmarks because it is your "last chance," are inadmissible. Make self-help, rather than dependence upon others, the watch-word of your career.

12. Next door to begging is borrowing, which is almost equally to be avoided. If you borrow anything, let it be only from intimate friends, and not from any casual acquaintance, and always be very careful to return the article borrowed as quickly as possible. Never borrow money from anybody if you can avoid doing so; but, if you do, to be careless about returning it is doubly inexcusable.

Do not fall into the habit of borrowing books; it is

better to buy them for yourself (if they are worth having), or to procure them from a lending library. People who value their books never much like to lend them; and to ask them to do so, unless you are on intimate terms with them, is a liberty which you are not justified in taking. Be very careful in your treatment of borrowed books, whether lent you by a friend or procured from a library; do not soil or dog's-ear them or make pencil notes or other marks in the margin. Finally, be very particular to return books borrowed from a friend to their owner within a reasonable time; do not keep them indefinitely, till he is obliged to ask for them back; it is your duty, not his, to see that they are returned.

13. Whatever kind of dress you wear, be clean and neat in your person and attire. Keep your finger-nails short and free from dirt. Be careful that there are no buttons missing from your shirt or your *chapkan*.

If you wear a "brimless cap" or skull-cup of any kind, see that it is not soiled with dust or grease; but, in your social intercourse with Europeans, it is better to wear either the *shamla* or the *mogli pagri*. On all official occasions "brimless caps" are inadmissible.[1]

Similarly, the neatest kind of shoes to wear are patent leather or ordinary black leather[2] shoes of European fashion with elastic sides; and such shoes are the most convenient for Indian gentlemen to wear at all public ceremonies and in visiting at European houses; in short,

---

[1] Government of Bengal Resolution (Political), dated 30th January, 1880.

[2] If these are worn, they require to be polished with shoe-blacking; Indian gentlemen are too apt to forget this.

in English society generally. If you wear the loose-fitting Indian shoe, to keep it on the foot in the houses of Europeans, is an act of discourtesy towards them. Shoes of Indian fashion must be taken off on all official or semi-official occasions.[1]

In European society (as, at dinners or Garden Parties), it is more convenient to wear trousers than to wear the *dhoti*. At places of public promenade, &c., where Europeans and especially where European ladies are present, if the *dhoti* be worn, it should be of sufficient length to cover the legs decently, and stockings, rather than socks, should be worn. If you wear the *dhoti*, you should be the more chary of lolling and lounging (see Rule 3), since the display of bare leg that may be caused by such attitudes is particularly ungraceful.

Avoid a tendency to display or foppishness in clothing or adorning your person. Dress according to your rank, without extravagance. Prefer neatness to gaudiness.

If you wear European dress, be sober in your attire, and avoid staring colours or patterns.

Similarly, do not overload your fingers with rings or wear a very massive gold watch-chain. English gentlemen wear no other jewellery than studs, sleeve-links, a watch and chain of moderate size, a scarf-pin, and seldom more than one ring[2] (a signet-ring), which is placed on the little finger. Never wear false jewellery.

If you wear spectacles or an eye-glass, let them be of light make, mounted in gold or blue steel, and fastened by a thin black silk cord or thread.

---

[1] Government of India Resolution No. 514, dated 19th March, 1868.

[2] Two, at most.

Pocket-handkerchiefs should be of white cambric, or white or red silk, or cambric bordered with red or purple silk.

Above all, the shirt-front should be perfectly plain, not laced or embroidered in any way.

Descriptions of dress, whether European or Indian, suitable for various occasions, will be found under their respective headings.

CHAPTER II.

CALLS.

CALLS made by Indian gentlemen upon Europeans are usually of two kinds: (1) ceremonious or semi-ceremonious calls, and (2) calls on business; but the ceremonious call (or call "to pay his respects") is often, to the convenience of both parties, utilised for a matter of business.

A call made upon an English lady is generally, however, a strictly ceremonious call, and the caller should be careful not to introduce into his conversation with the wife any business matter that he may have with the husband.

In India a European gentleman who has newly come to a town or a station, calls on the residents *first*, without waiting for them to call on him. They will then return his call. If he comes to a large city, as Calcutta, where it is scarcely possible for him to call on all the residents, he would call on those whom he specially wished to know, or on those who were in his own Department of the Public Service. He might also suitably call on any residents whom he had previously met at entertainments to which he had been invited.

Such is the etiquette of calling with Europeans in India; and, similarly, Indian gentlemen, on arriving at a new station, should be the first to call upon any Europeans that they wished to become acquainted with.

But it is not at present usual for Europeans to call upon Indian gentlemen at their houses,[1] unless they live in the European fashion and their wives receive callers. Consequently Indian gentlemen must, as a rule, (whether they are new arrivals or not) be the first to call on any Europeans they desire to know, and will not expect their calls to be returned.

Such ceremonious calls are usually made upon a Government official when he first comes to settle in a station; and they may be repeated at intervals of six months or a year. They may also be made on any special occasion, such as when the visitor or the person visited is about to leave the station permanently or for a long time, or when either of them has returned to the station after a long absence.

After any entertainment to which you have received an invitation, it is etiquette to call upon your host and hostess as an acknowledgment of their kindness. This should be done within a week, at most, after the entertainment, and whether the proffered invitation has been accepted or declined.

If you have been invited to a wedding (besides calling upon those who gave the wedding entertainment), it is your duty to call upon the bride and bridegroom, as soon as they have returned from their wedding trip or tour.

If a European gentleman of your acquaintance is ill or is suffering under any domestic affliction (such as family sickness or bereavement), and you wish to show

---

[1] Because it is not usually convenient for Indian gentlemen to receive European callers at their houses.

your concern or sympathy, do not call, but leave your card at the house, with the words "To inquire" written in the upper left-hand corner. The recipient of such an attention, as soon as the crisis of his illness or affliction is over, will acknowledge it by sending you his card in return, with the words "With thanks (*or* To return thanks) for kind inquiries" written above his name.

If you call with a Letter of Introduction to your host (see p. 91), you should send the letter in along with your card by the servant, so that your host may be able to read the letter and find out who you are, before seeing you.

But it is perhaps better to send such letters by messenger or by post than to bring them personally. In the case of the Viceroy, Governor, Lieutenant-Governor, or other Head of a Province, Letters of Introduction should be sent to his Aide-de-Camp or Private Secretary.

If you wish to call on a lady or a gentleman who is staying in another gentleman's house, you should send in one card for the guest with "For Mr. (or Mrs.) Brown" (or whatever the name may be) written in ink or pencil at the top. You must, at the same time, leave cards for the host and hostess as well; though, if you are previously unacquainted with them, you will not necessarily see them, or only for a short time, it being understood that your call is meant chiefly for the guest. If the guest on whom you call has his wife with him (or *vice versâ*), you must send in two cards, one for each of them.

Calls are also made for the purpose of bidding good-bye to your friends, when you are about to leave the neighbourhood altogether or for a long period. In the case of only a temporary absence, farewell calls are unnecessary. When you make such calls, write *P. P. C.* in the lower right-hand corner of your card. The letters mean *Pour prendre congé*, which is French for "To take leave." It is permissible to send such cards by post, instead of leaving them in person.

In all other cases, cards must be left by the caller in person, and must not be sent by post, or delivered by a messenger, or left by a friend.

From 12 to 2 o'clock in the day is the ceremonious hour for calling in India ; and if the call is made upon a lady, these hours should be strictly adhered to. If, however, the call is made upon a gentleman at his office, some time between the hours of 11 A.M. and 1-30 P.M., or between 3 and 4-30 P.M., is generally the most convenient for a call. If the call is made at his house, it is better to make it *before* rather than *after* office hours : an Indian gentleman calling at 4 or 5 P.M. is apt to interfere with the rest or recreation of his host.[1]

Both in Calcutta and the Mofussil, Sunday is the day on which European gentlemen generally pay calls to ladies, always between 12 and 2 o'clock ; but it is perhaps better for an Indian gentleman to choose some other day for his visit, as the lady is then less likely to be taken up with other callers, and he will be able to make or renew his acquaintance with her more easily. As regards the gentleman of the house, Sunday is a day on which he will probably be found at home between 12 and 4, but most English gentlemen object

---

[1] In the Mof. ssil, office hours are often in the early morning, and calls must be regulated accordingly.

to be interrupted on that day by ceremonious or business matters.

If the call is on the lady of the house, you necessarily call on her husband as well, though you may probably not see him. Send in, therefore, two cards by the servant before entering the house. If your call is made upon the gentleman only, one card is sufficient; and it will then be understood that your card is meant for him alone.

Modern English taste requires that a visiting-card should be plain and unostentatious; it should be made of white *unglazed* and not very stiff card-board. The name should be printed upon it in black (not in gold) in small clear copper-plate, without flourishes; or it may be clearly written on a blank card.

It is best to give your full name and designation or title on your visiting-card: as, *Babu Dwarka Nath Mitter, Moulvie Muhammed Sultan Alum, Raja Ramanath Tagore.* The title of "Honourable" is the only title that is never given on a visiting-card.

Some Indian gentlemen use the English designation *Mr.;* and, if they prefer it, there is no objection to the practice. Add, in writing, to your name your official or other designation; so that your host may know at once who you are. But do not have such designations *printed* on your card. If you are a University Graduate, do not place B.A., M.A., M.B., &c., after your name on your visiting card. But if you have a professional title, it should precede your name on your card; as, *Dr. Kali Nath Gupta.* It is better not to omit the prefix of "Babu" or "Mr.," &c., before the name. Your address should be written or printed in the lower left-hand corner of the card.

If you are calling by appointment, you may find it useful to write "By appointment" on the margin of your card above your name, so as to recall the circumstance to the mind of your host. Should you be requested to write your business upon a slate or upon the back of your card, do so as quickly and concisely as possible.

If you are not supplied with a card, write your name, &c., neatly on a clean slip of paper or on the slate provided in some houses. But when the call is made on a lady, a card is indispensable. *Never enter the presence of your host unannounced.* Even if you should be on such very intimate terms with your host as to be able to dispense with sending in your name, always knock at the room door before you enter.

If the lady or the gentleman on whom you are calling is too busy or too unwell to see you[1] or is not at home, you can leave your card or cards and retire; but if you desire to see them or make their acquaintance, do not leave any card, but take an opportunity of calling again.

Introductions are seldom made during calls, so that if the Indian visitor finds other callers in the room when he enters the presence of his host or hostess, he should not feel surprised or offended if he is not introduced to them. If, however, in the course of conversation, occasion should arise, he may address a remark to another caller without having been previously introduced to him. But such an occurrence does not at all necessi-

[1] In the case of a lady, the durwan will inform you that "the door is shut" (*durwaza bund*): a formula which means that she is unable to receive callers.

tate that an acquaintance should be afterwards acknowledged between them.

Be careful not to make your visit too long. A ceremonious or complimentary call should not be extended to more than ten minutes at most. If the call is on business, it may last somewhat longer according to the requirements of the case, but should not be unnecessarily protracted, as the time of all classes of Europeans in India is valuable.

Do not, therefore, be afraid to come to your business at once, or with but a short introduction. Avoid prefacing any request you have to make, or favour you have to ask, with set speeches or elaborate compliments. Let your statement of the case be brief and to the point; and do not waste the time of your host with a long conversation about nothing in particular, and then, when he is getting wearied, and the interview is drawing to a close, at last introduce the business matter about which you have come, as if it were a sort of afterthought. Your host will be quite intelligent enough to perceive that the business matter is the main object of your call, and will inwardly regret that you did not bring it forward at the beginning of your visit.

Do not repeat a complimentary visit except after a considerable interval of time. Officials and most other Europeans in India are busy men, and have little leisure. For the same reason, if your call is by appointment, it is important to be punctual.

If the call is made upon a lady, the Indian gentleman should be specially careful about his attire. If he wears the Indian dress, trousers of some kind are advisable;

and if loose Indian shoes, whether gold-laced or otherwise, are worn, he should leave them in his carriage or at the entrance of the house (see p. 11). But socks or stockings are necessary, since it is not polite to appear in a lady's presence with bare feet. For head-dress, the *shamla* or *mogli pagri* (see p. 10), or, in the case of Muhammedan gentlemen, an embroidered cap, should be worn, together with *choga* and *chapkan* [1]. This attire, or this with slight variations, also answers to the European full or evening dress.

If European dress is worn, it should consist of white linen shirt with collar and coloured necktie, black cloth morning (or frock) coat, black or white morning waistcoat, and coloured cloth (not tweed) trousers, with black boots or shoes. In the Presidency towns, a tall silk hat is indispensable; but in the Mofussil a round felt hat is generally worn. Gloves are not usually worn at calls in India [2]. On entering, take off your hat and carry it with you into the drawing-room. Be as ceremonious as possible in your dress; the apparel, especially in a lady's eyes, oft proclaims the man; but, above all, be absolutely clean and neat.

In an unceremonious call upon a gentleman, the *dhoti* may be worn and a velvet cap may take the place of the more formal head-dress.

---

[1] This description will not, of course, apply to all Indian gentlemen, whose customs in dress vary with their race, &c. But all should wear their most *formal* attire on such occasions.

[2] Should gloves be worn, they must be of kid, and the right hand glove must be removed before shaking hands with the lady on whom the call is made.

It is etiquette for a gentleman to take his silk umbrella or walking cane with him into the drawing-room; but if you carry a common sun umbrella or a rough stick, it is better to leave it in the porch, and not to take it with you into the room.

If you walk to the house, at entering wipe your shoes carefully on the door-mat. If you wear Indian shoes, leave them behind at the door-step or in the verandah; and be careful never to take off your turban or other Indian head-dress either before or during the interview.

Always remain seated in your carriage outside the house door till the servant who has taken your card returns with a *salaam* from his master or mistress. If you are on foot, wait outside under the portico till you receive the summons to enter. If there should happen to be no servant in attendance, search for one, or call "Bearer!" or "Durwan!" not too loudly. But do not enter the house till the servant has brought back his master's or mistress's invitation for you to enter. As soon as the servant, after presenting your card or cards, returns with a *salaam*, step in quietly without a noisy tread. If you have to go upstairs, walk up gently, lest you find yourself out of breath and hardly able to speak when you get to the top. When you enter the drawing-room, your host or hostess will rise and bow or shake hands with you. Do not be the first to offer your hand; wait till she holds out hers to you, then be ready to take it at once. If your host and hostess are both present, remember that the lady is always to be saluted first, and then the gentleman.

In shaking hands, take the hand firmly, grasping the hand and not the fingers merely, give it a gentle pressure and shake, and then relinquish it. Do not lift the hand up to shake, nor let it drop suddenly; and do not give a violent, or, on the other hand, a limp, nerveless shake; avoid squeezing the hand hard; and do not retain it in your own, giving intermittent shakes. Always *look* at the person with whom you shake hands.

When you are asked to sit down, take a seat quietly and gracefully and near to your host or hostess. Make yourself easy and comfortable; and do not sit on the extreme edge of your chair, or think to show a modest or respectful demeanour by trying to contract yourself into the smallest possible compass; but, at the same time, be careful not to loll or jog up and down in your seat, and avoid crossing your legs.

In conversing with your host or hostess, do not talk too loud or too fast; speak distinctly, but in a subdued tone. Cultivate a frank, quiet, and dignified manner; be cheerful without being hilarious. Show that you wish to be pleasant and polite, but do not be apologetic in your demeanour or over-anxious to chime in with the statements or opinions of the other party. Speak plainly and naturally, and avoid fine phrases or profuse compliments. Let your respect or esteem be shown by your manner rather than by your words. Remember that all open flattery is distasteful to the Anglo-Saxon temperament.

While you are right to show a proper interest in your host's affairs, avoid anything like inquisitiveness, and do not question him, for instance, about his age or the amount of his salary, or private, domestic, or official matters. If your curiosity is roused upon any subject, keep it under restraint; and if your interlocutor is reticent about the matter, forbear to question him. Leave him to communicate to you what he thinks fit, and never press questions upon him. Avoid, generally, awkward or unseasonable inquiries. Thus, if you are presented with a watch, do not ask the giver how much it cost.

Do not be too ready to talk of yourself or your belongings, unless in response to inquiries from your host or hostess.

Do not, again, when you meet your host (or hostess), and say "How do you do," make a practice of telling him how ill you think he is looking, or remark that he is thin or pale. Such solicitude, however complimentary in Indian society, is not considered so among Europeans, who, if they wish to please, tell one another how well, not how ill, they are looking.

Conversation during ceremonious calls should be of a light and general character. Avoid long arguments or discussions and learned or technical subjects, and do not keep to one topic. Do not interrupt a speaker by beginning to talk when he is in the middle of a sentence; wait till he has finished, and then introduce your remark. Do not monopolise the conversation; to listen well is as important as to talk well. If you tell an anecdote, let it be short and to the point.

In conversing with men or women of rank, do not give them their titles too frequently. It is well, however, for the visitor to show that he remembers the station of his interlocutor by now and then introducing some such phrase as "I think your Excellency was observing," or "As I was just telling your Honour." If the interview is a short one, it is sufficient to introduce the title once at its commencement.

In using other designations such as *General*, *Colonel*, *Doctor*, *Archdeacon*, always append the surname, unless you are on intimate terms with your interlocutor: as, "How do you do, Colonel Jones?" not "How do you do, Colonel?" "I hope you are well, Doctor Brown," not "I hope you are well, Doctor[1]." As a rule, however, names and titles should be introduced but little in conversation. *Sir*, *Madam*, and *Miss* (without the surname) are seldom or never used by English people in social converse as modes of address.

But in addressing the Head of a Province or Administration or any other person to whom special respect should be shown (as when an undergraduate is addressing his tutor or professor), it is proper to introduce the word *Sir* occasionally. Thus, in replying to a question, it would be polite to say "Yes, Sir" or "No, Sir," rather than plain "Yes" or "No."

As regards the colloquial application of titles—if you were speaking to the Queen, you would address her as *Your Majesty*, and a Royal Prince or Princess as *Your Royal Highness*. A Duke should be addressed as *Your Grace*, and a Marquis, an Earl, a Viscount, or a Baron, as *My Lord* or *Your Lordship*. An Archbishop is in conversation entitled *Your Grace*, and a Bishop *My Lord*.

When it is time to withdraw after your visit, do not wait to be dismissed or ask whether you may "take

---

[1] Do not omit the title altogether; see pp. 5, 6.

your leave[1]:" this is the Indian, but not the European, custom. The visitor should make the first move towards the termination of the interview. But, at the same time, do not act abruptly or rise to go when your entertainer is in the middle of a sentence; to do so would look as if you were tired of listening to his (or her) talk. Take the opportunity of a pause in the conversation to rise; offer your hand, and bid him (or her) good morning.

You may, at the same time, introduce some incidental remark so as not to make your departure appear too formal. Thus, to a lady you might say, "I am afraid I must be going," and to a gentleman, "I fear I am trespassing upon your time," or words to that effect.

After shaking hands with you, a lady will generally remain where she is; a gentleman will often accompany you to the room door (especially if he is on intimate or friendly terms with you) and there your final adieux will be made by mutual bows; do not expect or offer to shake hands after the interview more than once.

If other visitors arrive or depart in the course of your call, it is polite to rise when they enter or leave the room. This should *always* be done when the other visitors are ladies.

If after having been ushered into a room, you have to await the appearance of your host (or hostess), take a chair and remain seated till he (or she) enters. Do not wander about the room, in the interval, on a tour of inspection, and finger ornaments or other articles.

---

[1] When the visit is made to a high official (as to a Lieutenant-Governor), it is etiquette to ask permission to withdraw (see p. 69); but in the case of ordinary calls it is unnecessary to do so.

CHAPTER III.

BALLS, EVENING PARTIES, AT HOMES, INTRODUCTIONS.

INDIAN gentlemen are not usually invited to balls unless they have adopted European social customs, and so regard dancing from a European point of view.

Balls generally commence at nine or half-past nine o'clock in the evening. There is, however, no necessity to be punctual, unless you have previously engaged yourself to dance in the early part of the evening ; otherwise, you may arrive an hour late, if you prefer to do so.

At a ball, never think of attempting to dance, unless you know the step, and have learnt to dance properly.

If you do not dance, you can stand on one side or in a doorway and look on at the dancing, or you can sit in any seats that may be provided and converse with your friends. But be very careful not to get in the way of those who are dancing. The object of a ball is dancing, not lounging about ; and the dancers are to have the first consideration.

If candles, whether in chandeliers or in Chinese lanterns, are used for lighting a ball-room, precautions should be taken that the wax may not drop on the dresses or coats of those present. Do not hang up a Chinese lantern immediately over a doorway through which people pass.

At private balls, the guests are received by the hostess at the head of the staircase, who shakes hands with each guest on arrival. But if you arrive late, she may be otherwise engaged, and it is then your duty to seek her out, and pay your respects to her.

Full or evening dress, whether European or Indian, is to be worn at balls, evening parties, and evening *At Homes.* European dress-clothes consist of trousers, open-fronted waistcoat, and swallow-tailed coat—all of black broadcloth, with white linen shirt (see p. 12), white cambric neck-tie, and patent-leather boots or shoes [1]. For Indian full dress, see pp. 19, 20. At balls, white (or light lavender, or pale yellow) kid gloves must also be worn with European evening dress, and white, instead of black, waistcoats are permissible. Gloves are not usually worn with Indian full dress; but for a gentleman who wishes to dance they are indispensable.

You need not take your card of invitation with you to private balls, *At Homes*, &c., or to any State entertainments (unless it should be notified on the card that you are to do so). At all public balls people take with them their cards of admission.

Ante-rooms, one for gentlemen, and another for ladies (the one for ladies being furnished with a looking-glass, &c.,) are provided for the deposit of outer coats or wrappings, none of which are, on any account, to be taken into the ball-room.

If an Indian gentleman wishes to give a ball, an evening party, or an *At Home*, he should issue his invitations about three weeks beforehand. An invitation to a ceremonious ball is printed in black or in gold on

---

[1] If *shoes* are worn, black or red silk socks are necessary.

large-sized cards; and a monogram or crest may be added in the centre at the top of the card, which may be gilt-edged, if desired. Thus:—

THE MAHARAJAH OF DINAPORE
requests the honour of
MR. & MRS. A. B. BROWN'S
company at a Ball
on Monday, January 4th,
at half-past nine o'clock.

RAJBATI;
December 12, 1886. } *R. S. V. P.*

All this is printed except the name of the guest or guests. The letters *R. S. V. P.* mean *Répondez s'il vous plait,* which is French for "Answer, if you please." If the ball is to take place at some public building, as a Town Hall, the words "at the Town Hall" should be added after the word "Ball." If the ceremonious entertainment consists of an Evening Party the words "an Evening Party" in place of "a Ball" is all the change required.

If the Ball or Party is given in honour of some distinguished personage, as a Royal Prince, the words, "To have the honour of meeting H. R. H. the Duke of Connaught" (or whoever it may be) should be written or printed at the top of the card.

If the entertainment is not on a grand and formal scale, the invitation should be issued on *At Home* cards of a smaller size, the monogram or crest being retained, if desired. The words "Dancing," "Music," "Private Theatricals," &c., according to the nature of the entertainment, are added in the lower right hand corner, the letters *R. S. V. P.* being placed below them.[1] The name of the guest or guests is written at the top of the card. Thus:—

MR. A. M. ROBINSON.

BABU CHANDRA CHARAN GHOSE
At Home,
Tuesday, December 21st,
at 9 o'clock.

120, Chowringhee. Dancing.
R. S. V. P.

All this is usually printed except the name of the guest, the date, and hour, and the word "Dancing;" or, if the cards are specially printed for the occasion, only the guest's name appears in writing.

Since, however, entertainments given by Indian gentlemen to Europeans are usually formal affairs, it will be better for them, as a rule, to use the more formal style of invitation.

An invitation to a Conversazione will run as follows, the whole being printed except the name of the guest:—

THE ISLAM LITERARY SOCIETY
requests the pleasure of
MR. H. L. JONES'S
company at a Conversazione
in the Society's Rooms, 109, Park Street,
on Monday, the 10th February, at 9 p.m.

MUHAMMED ALUM KHAN,
Hony. Secretary.

The Secretary's name need not be printed, if he prefers to append his own signature.

---

[1] Or they may be omitted, since answers are often not required to invitations of this kind. It is also unnecessary to append the letters to invitations to Meetings, Prize-Distributions, &c.

In all these invitations, the expression "requests the pleasure" is less formal than "requests the honour." The latter should, therefore, be used on occasions of ceremony.

A few other forms of invitation are added :—

(1.) WELLESLEY DEBATING CLUB.
The President and Committee
request the honour of
MR. H. M. SMITH'S
presence at their
ANNUAL MEETING
at the Ripon Hall, 59, Wellesley Street,
on Friday, the 30th instant, at 6 p.m.
The Hon'ble Mr. Justice EVANS will preside.

(2.) BABU KALI MOHUN ROY
requests the honour of the
HON'BLE A. L. THOMSON'S
company on the occasion of the
DISTRIBUTION OF PRIZES
at the Roy School, 231, Circular Road,
on Saturday, the 4th of March, at 4-30 p.m.
The Commissioner of the Presidency Division has kindly consented to preside.

Do not say "*to witness* the distribution" (or whatever the ceremony may be), but "*on the occasion of* the distribution," as above; or simply "presence (instead of *company*) at the distribution."

(3.) *To have the honour of meeting H. E. the Viceroy.*
THE MAHARAJAH OF RAMPORE
requests the honour of the
HON'BLE SIR GEORGE AND LADY JONES'S
company on the occasion of the ceremony of laying the Foundation-Stone of the Ripon Institute, on Monday, the 10th of April, at 5 p.m., and afterwards at an *At Home.*

R. S. V. P.

(4.) The Committee
of the
GRANT HOSPITAL BUILDING FUND
request the honour of
MR. A. B. BROWN'S
presence at the ceremony of the laying of the
FOUNDATION-STONE
of the Hospital by
HIS HONOUR THE LIEUTENANT-GOVERNOR
on Monday, the 10th instant, at 5-30 p.m.

(5.) *Durga Poojah.*
MAHARAJAH KALI KRISHNA
AND
BABU NILMANI KRISHNA
present their compliments to
G. W. FENN, ESQ.,
and request the honour of his company at
PRIVATE THEATRICALS
to be held at their house on 23rd, 24th, and 25th instant, at 9-30 p.m.
RAMBAZAR RAJBATI;[1]
The 5th Sept. 1887.

In drawing up and printing invitation cards, care should be taken that the invitations are correctly worded, and that they contain no grammatical blunders or printers' errors. Indian gentlemen are often careless on this point, forgetting that such carelessness is really a form of impoliteness. It is much like writing *Yrs.* for *Yours* at the end of a letter. Mind, for instance, that *request* and not *requests* is printed on the card, if the subject of the verb is in the plural number; and if the *'s* is not printed on the card, see that it is appended to the name of the guest before the word "company."

[1] Do not write "Maharajah Kali Krishna's" *place; place* thus used is slang.

Words like "presents his respectful compliments and requests" instead of the simple form "requests," are unnecessary, unless great formality of expression is desired.

At balls honoured by the presence of a member of the Royal Family or the Viceroy or some other distinguished personage, or if the ball is given in honour of some particular individual, it is etiquette to wait for the arrival of such "guests of the evening" before dancing commences.

Such a guest would open the ball by dancing a Quadrille with his hostess or with the lady of highest rank present.

If a Royal Princess were present, she would open the ball with her host, if he were accustomed to dance.

Royal or Viceregal guests (or other guests of special distinction) should always be received by their host at the entrance of the house, and be by him conducted to the ball or assembly room.

Such guests would shake hands with their host, who should make a low bow. A Royal Princess would enter the ball-room leaning on the arm of her host.

The same etiquette should be observed on the departure of such guests as on their arrival.

Introductions to such guests are made only at their own request.

At parties of this kind, if you are the host, do not try to introduce everybody to everybody else. Introduce those among your guests to each other to whom you consider that such an introduction would be welcome. In the same way, if you are a guest, do not expect to be introduced to everyone present. If you wish to become acquainted with another guest, who, you think, would like to know you, apply to your hostess (or host) for an introduction.

Do not force yourself into people's notice, and if you have been in society with a gentleman of higher social position than your own, leave it to him at a subsequent meeting to speak first or to recognise you. As a general rule, it is the place of the superior in rank to speak first to the inferior.

But if you should find an agreeable person in private society, who seems desirous of making your acquaintance, there can be no objection to your meeting his advances half-way, although the ceremony of an "introduction" may not have taken place. But in the case of a lady (unless she addresses you), never speak to her without a previous introduction.

Similarly, if you are a dancing man, do not offer to dance with a lady without first obtaining an introduction to her, which may be done through a common friend or through certain persons appointed to act as "Stewards", whose business it is to look after these matters. But do not, on any account, go up to a strange lady by yourself and ask her to dance, as she will unhesitatingly "decline the honour."

Remember that a presentation to a lady in a ball-room for the purpose of dancing, does not entitle you to claim her acquaintance afterwards.

In making an introduction between two people, say to the person of higher rank, "Sir John (*or* Lady) Brown, allow me to introduce to you Babu Kali Mohun Roy." Then say, "Babu Kali Mohun Roy—Sir John Brown."

Do not repeat the names in reverse order; *once* naming the names of those who are to be introduced to each other is enough.

In speaking the two names, remember to put the name of the person of lower rank *first*, if both the persons are of the same sex. If, however, the introduction is between a lady and a gentleman, the gentleman's name must always come first, since it is the gentleman that is introduced to the lady, not the lady to the gentleman. Thus, "The Maharajah of Rampore—Mrs. Brown;" *not* "Mrs. Brown—The Maharajah of Rampore."

When the presentation has been made, the two guests will bow and say "How do you do?" to each other, and if they are both gentlemen, will generally shake hands. Ladies do not usually shake hands with a gentleman on the first introduction, though it is quite etiquette for them to do so if they wish.

If you are being introduced to a lady (or to a gentleman of higher rank than your own), do not offer to shake hands with her unless she first holds out her hand to you.

If the introduction is to a gentleman of lower rank than your own, you are at liberty to be the first to offer to shake hands, should you wish to appear friendly.

After the presentation, the two guests will generally make some civil speech to each other, such as "I am very happy to make your acquaintance," and join in a friendly conversation.

If your host or hostess should happen unknowingly to introduce you to some one with whom you are not on friendly terms, the two guests so introduced should make a slight bow to each other, no further communication being necessary. The bow is a courtesy due to your host or hostess to avoid unpleasantness under their roof, and the two guests may pass each other without recognition afterwards.

When the time for supper arrives, the host should offer his *right* arm to the lady of highest rank and lead off to the supper-room. A few ladies and gentleman next in rank would follow. Afterwards the rest of the guests would go to supper as they pleased, quite irrespective of rank or anything but their desire to be together.

But, until the host has set the example, no guest should venture to make for the supper-room, and by so doing cause a general move in that direction.

If the Viceroy, Governor, &c., or a Royal personage be present, all the guests remain standing till such personages have taken their seats at the supper-table. Similarly, when they rise from the table, it is etiquette for all the guests to rise at the same time and remain standing till they have quitted the supper-room. Afterwards any guests may leave it or resume their seats if they have not finished supper.

At large evening parties and *At Homes*, refreshments are generally provided at buffets or side tables, near which the guests stand and take what they require at any time they please.

A gentleman escorting a lady to the supper-room should remain with her all the time she stays there. He should also return with her to the ball-room, unless her partner for the next dance arrives to remind her of the engagement, in which case the gentleman who had taken her to supper would make her a bow and resign her to the other gentleman, with whom she would return to the ball-room.

As soon as he reaches the supper-room, a gentleman should remove his gloves, putting them on again after supper is over.

If Royal or Viceregal or other highly distinguished personages are present at the entertainment, do not try to thrust yourself under their notice, by edging near them or standing just in front of them. Do not stare at them, or whisper or point at them, or push past your neighbours in order to get a front place and a good view of them. However desirous you may be of seeing any celebrity, do not display any hurry or excitement, but be quiet and dignified in your bearing.

At balls and large entertainments where many guests are present, it is not etiquette for the guests, on their departure, to take leave of their host or hostess. But if the party is on a comparatively small scale, it is right to do so.

If you are a guest at an evening party given by a European at his private residence, either Indian or European full or evening dress (see p. 27) should be worn; or, if you do not possess the Indian full dress, wear what clothes you have that are the nearest approach to it, and let them at least be clean and neat. Trousers, however, and shoes of European pattern had better be worn. It is not etiquette to wear gloves when there is no dancing.

As in case of a dinner party (see p. 43), on arriving, leave your stick or umbrella or any outer wrappings, such as a woollen comforter or shawl, in the entrance hall. Do not think of carrying them with you into the drawing-room.

At evening parties or other entertainments, if you politely wish to provide any one with a seat, do not offer him or her the chair from which you have just risen, unless there is no other to be had.

On entering, shake hands first with your hostess, who will be ready to receive you, and then with your host, if he is at hand, unless he has previously greeted you outside the room. You can afterwards bow to or shake hands with any other acquaintances or friends that may be present.

While being chary of thrusting yourself forward, you are at liberty to fall into conversation with any one who may be near you, without waiting for a formal introduction. The fact that you and the other guests are under the same roof is introduction enough; and it is no breach of etiquette, but rather an act of politeness, to address some pleasant remarks to your neighbours, if it is done naturally. This does not, of course, mean that you should go abruptly up to somo stranger present and insist on conversing with him, whether he wishes it or not.

Mix, then, freely with the company and join in the conversation or in any amusement that may be provided. Avoid, as far as possible, crowding into a corner with your associates. Take advantage of such social gatherings to learn something of European ways and habits of thought and feeling in private life, away from the office and the lecture-room. You cannot begin to sympathise till you begin to understand; and when you have got over the first strangeness of your surroundings (if you have never been a guest at such parties before), you will soon find that you are among those who wish to treat you with friendliness and geniality.

Hence, do all you can to second their endeavours, and be ready to enter gently and quietly into any game or other pastime that may be arranged for or suggested by your host or hostess.

If you do not object on religious grounds to partaking of the refreshments provided, do so in moderation ; but wait till you are asked, or till the servants bring them round to you. You can, of course, consult your own wishes entirely as to whether you take such refreshments or not. You will transgress no rule of etiquette by not doing so. It will be the wish of your entertainers that you should, as far as may be, enjoy yourself in your own way.

Remember that in English society ladies are treated with the greatest attention and politeness. Thus if a lady drops her fan, handkerchief, or other article, it is good manners to pick it up for her at once ; and if she makes a movement to do anything that you can do for her (as to fetch a footstool or draw up a chair), it is polite to anticipate her wishes with the words, "Allow me."

Evening parties usually break up about 11 o'clock, or sometimes a little later. But do not take your leave till the lady of highest rank (or the gentleman of highest rank, if there are no ladies present) has done so, when the company will make a general move to go. Then shake hands in your turn with your hostess (or host), and say, "Good-night, Mrs. (*or* Mr.) Jones."

Do not think it necessary to go round and shake hands with all the guests at parting. You will naturally bid good-night to those near you, and shake hands with those who appear desirous of doing so. Otherwise a bow is sufficient.

Leave the house quietly without noise or clatter or the slightest display of hilarity. Your host will generally bid you farewell at the door, and will see that you are provided with any coat or shawl that you have left below.

In bidding farewell to your host at the door, if you have enjoyed the party, it will not be out of place to say, "We have had a delightful evening," or words to that effect; but it is well to avoid any *formal* expression of gratitude for the hospitality you have received.

CHAPTER IV.

DINNER-PARTIES AND DINING OUT.

In Anglo-Indian Society, invitations to dinner-parties are usually made by letter, written by the hostess, to whom, even if the invitation is written by the host, the answer should always be addressed.[1] Such an invitation would run thus:—

Dear Mrs. Brown,

Will you and your husband give us the pleasure of your company at dinner on Thursday, March 3rd, at 8 o'clock?

3, Park Lane; Yours sincerely,
Wednesday. Mary Jones.

The reply, in case of acceptance, would be:—

Dear Mrs. Jones,

My husband and I have much pleasure in accepting your kind invitation to dinner on Thursday, March 3rd.

2, Grant Street; Yours sincerely,
Wednesday. Louisa M. Brown.

In case of refusal:—

Dear Mrs. Jones,

My husband and I much regret that a previous engagement prevents us from accepting your kind invitation to dinner on Thursday.

2, Grant Street; Yours sincerely,
Wednesday. Louisa M. Brown.

Some, however, use printed cards of invitation; and Indian gentlemen, giving formal dinners to Europeans,

---

[1] *Never* use the vulgar contraction, "invite."

will find it best to use such cards, since they are more ceremonious. In cases where the lady of the house mixes in European society, the names of both the host and hostess should figure on the invitation card; otherwise, the name of the host alone is sufficient. Thus:—

MR. and MRS. CHUCKERBUTTY
request the pleasure of
MR. and MRS. A. B. BROWN'S
company at dinner, on
Monday, April 4th,
at 8 o'clock.

104, Chowringhee Road;
March 21st, 1887.

All this is printed except the names of those giving the dinner and of their guests, and the dates and hour. The verb *request* must, of course, be put in the singular number (*requests*) if the name of the host alone figures on the card. Should the entertainment be a specially ceremonious one, the whole may be printed except, of course, the names of the guests; and a crest or monogram in gold may be placed at the top of the card (which should then be of a larger size), together with the letters *R.S.V.P.* (see p. 28) at the bottom right-hand corner.

In the case of a dinner given by an Indian gentleman to European guests, the Indian host should be present at table even if he does not partake of the meal. It is not polite for him to sit apart in another room till the dinner is over, unless, indeed, he has caste scruples on the subject.

If the dinner is a large and formal one, the invitations should be sent out at least a fortnight before the date of the dinner; otherwise, a week or ten days' notice is sufficient.

Those who are invited should reply *immediately* (on the same day on which they receive the invitation, if possible). It shows the greatest want of courtesy to let a lady (or gentleman) wait to know whether her invitation is accepted or not. The answer too must not be a doubtful one; the invitation must be unreservedly accepted or declined. The answer should be written thus, in case of acceptance :—

MR. and MRS. A. B. BROWN have much pleasure in accepting MR. and MRS. CHUCKERBUTTY'S kind invitation to dinner on Monday, April 4th.

50, Park Street,
March 22nd, 1887.

In case of refusal, thus:—

MR. and MRS. A. B. BROWN much regret that, owing to a previous engagement, they are unable to accept &c.

In India, invitations and replies are usually sent by a *chuprasi*, who carries a peon-book in which receipt of either is acknowledged; but it is permissible to send them by post.

Every engagement, and especially a dinner engagement, is sacred, and should never be broken except for very weighty reasons.

If, after accepting an invitation, unforeseen circumstances (as illness) should prevent you from fulfilling your engagement, you must *at once* let your hostess (or host) know, expressing your great regret at the occurrence.

It is customary, in India, for guests to bring their own servants with them to wait upon them at table. You should, therefore, tell your servant beforehand when and where you are dining out, that he may be there to attend upon you. At some houses, however, waiters at table are provided by the host, and no outside servants are admitted. But tell your servant, in any case, the date and place of the dinner; he will find out for himself whether his attendance is required or not.

An Indian gentleman of position, in giving a dinner or supper-party to Europeans, had better entrust the catering to some European hotel-manager or confectioner, who will see that it is served in proper style. He may arrange with his purveyor beforehand as to the kind of dinner or supper he wishes to give, whether a highly elaborate or a less formal one; but, whatever be the character of the entertainment, he should give orders that the wines provided be of the best description.

A guest must be careful to be punctual. It is very bad manners to keep your entertainer and his other guests waiting for your arrival; and the dinner is apt to be spoiled by delay. No gentleman guest would be waited for longer than a quarter of an hour; when that time had expired, the dinner would commence without him. A little more grace would be given to a lady guest, even to the extent of half-an-hour.

In dressing for a dinner of this kind, either European or Indian, full or evening dress must be worn (see p. 27). With neither description of dress are gloves to be worn at dinners. On arriving, if you are in European costume, leave your hat or cap, overcoat, &c., in the entrance hall. If you wear the Indian dress, do not remove your *pagrī*; but be careful to divest yourself of any outer wrappings. Be careful that your hands and finger-nails are scrupulously clean and neat.

On entering the drawing-room, your first duty is to shake hands with your hostess, or with your host if there is no lady of the house present; you would then stand and talk with any gentleman of your acquaintance present, or, if there is a lady near you whom you know, you might, after a bow of recognition, stand or take a seat beside her and talk to her. If you sit, it is polite to rise at the entrance of other guests.

If you are a stranger to those present, your entertainer will probably present you to some of the other guests; but introductions of all the guests to one another are not necessary or customary at dinner-parties.

If, at dinner, you happen to sit next to another guest to whom you have not been introduced, the fact that you are present at the same table is sufficient to warrant your addressing some pleasant remark to him or her, and you can enter into conversation with each other without committing any breach of etiquette.

If you are the host, you should advance and shake hands with each guest, as soon as he or she enters the drawing-room; if several guests enter together, greet the lady or ladies first, and afterwards the gentlemen. If the party is a large one, it is well to take your stand near the door, so as to be ready to welcome your guests without difficulty.

At a dinner-party in India, especially where ladies are present, precedence is of great importance. As soon as dinner is announced, the host must escort (by giving her his arm) the lady of highest rank, and they lead the way to the dining-room; those next in position are paired off together in succession; the hostess, escorted by the gentleman entitled to the highest precedence, bringing up the rear of the procession. There should always be at least as many gentlemen as there are ladies, so that no lady may be unescorted. No gentleman may escort two ladies. The host should go round, before dinner is announced, and tell each gentleman which lady he is to escort; and if he finds they are strangers to each other, he should take the gentleman up to the lady and introduce them to each other. At a formal dinner, if the guests are ignorant of one another's rank, and so do not know in what order they are to proceed to the dining-room, the host should, at the same time, tell each gentleman what his place is in the procession; whether he is 2nd, 3rd, 4th, &c. But at ordinary dinner-parties, this matter is left to the discretion of the guests. To prevent confusion, it is well for the host to have the names of the gentlemen and of the ladies they are to escort written on a slip of paper, so that he can refer to it in case of forgetfulness. In taking a lady down to dinner, the gentleman should give her his right arm.

Strict etiquette requires that a gentleman should place the lady he has escorted on his right hand at the dinner table. The host takes his seat at one end of the table, giving the seat on his right to the lady he has taken in, while the lady of the next rank seats herself on his left. The hostess sits at the opposite end of the table with the gentleman that has escorted her on her left. It is a good plan to place a small card, or china slab, bearing the name of each guest, behind the plate on the dinner-table at the place where he or she is to sit. In case of a large dinner-party, this should always be done, as it prevents much confusion.

Do not seat husband and wife next to each other or even opposite to each other, if you can avoid it ; and as far as the rules of precedence allow, endeavour to place congenial people next to one another.

The arrangement of the dinner-table and the *matériel* of the dinner itself is not enlarged upon here, as an Indian gentleman, who gives a dinner of this kind, would best entrust such matters to European direction. One or two hints, however, may be given on matters which are sometimes neglected.

The lighting of the dining-room is important to the comfort of the guests. The room must be well lighted, but the light should be thrown on the table, not in the eyes of the guests. Hence, if lamps or candles are placed on the dinner-table, they must be carefully shaded by coloured silk or paper shades. But it is perhaps better to have your lamps or candles suspended from the ceiling or placed high up on the walls ; and even then, shades are desirable, both to soften the glare and to throw the light below.

It is well to consult the comfort of your lady guests by placing footstools under the table opposite their chairs.

In the decoration of the dinner-table, do not allow tall plants or lofty epergnes to be placed upon it. All decorations should be low enough for the guests to see over them. When people have to crane their necks round bunches of flowers or over tall vases in order to see or converse with their opposite neighbours, the effect is the reverse of becoming or agreeable.

In India, no dishes, except fruit or conserves, are, as a rule, placed on the table; joints are carved by the butler in a side-room, and the plates of meat are handed round to the guests by the other servants. *Entrées* are always carried round for the guests to help themselves. Plates and dishes should be handed round to the guests in the order in which they are sitting,[1] beginning with the lady on the right hand of the host. If double *entrées* are provided, they would be handed round on either side of the table simultaneously. Only a moderate quantity of soup should be served to each guest; a plate full of soup is in very bad taste.

The order of viands at an ordinary dinner is—1, Soup; 2, Fish; 3, *Entrées* (or Side-dishes); 4, Joint (or Turkey);[2] 5, Second course (or *Sikkin*); 6, Pudding (or Sweets); 7, Cheese; 8, Ices; 9, Dessert. At ceremonious dinners, the soup is preceded by *hors d'œuvres*, or appetisers, such as anchovies, olives, caviare, &c.; and the *entrées* and sweets are more numerous and varied.

There is great art in eating properly. Transact all the business of the table quietly and gently. Do not eat quickly or ravenously, and never smack your lips. Take small mouthfuls, not large ones. Open your mouth just as your fork reaches your lips, not before. Do not rattle your knife, fork, and spoon, or make a clatter-

---

[1] Do not let your servants wander hither and thither round the table, from the notion that the ladies ought to be helped first.

[2] Or the joint may precede the *entrées*.

ing noise with them on your plate. Above all, do not make a noise in masticating your food, and keep your lips closed during the process. Avoid drinking anything or talking when your mouth is full; wait till you have finished what you have in your mouth. Do not drain your wine-glass to the last drop, or scrape your plate clean of every morsel of food upon it. Remember that a wine-glass is to be held by the stem, and not by the bowl.

It is etiquette to begin to eat any dish as soon as it is set before you; do not wait till others are helped. Do not think that you should abstain from taking the last piece of any dish; to do so implies a fear that your host has not made sufficient provision for his guests.

Do not partake of any dish more than once; it is not etiquette to ask for a second help, and should seldom or never be done outside the home circle. If you do not like a dish to which you have been helped, do not send away your plate at once, but take a mouthful or two, or at least make believe to do so, till you can have your plate removed without exciting observation.

Be careful how you sit at table. Do not sit leaning over on one side, or put your elbows on the table or on the back of your neighbour's chair, or twist restlessly about. Sit in an upright, but at the same time easy, position.

Beware of gaping, and if you fall into a yawn unawares, place your hand before your mouth, and ask your neighbour's pardon for indulging in it. People are more particular about matters of this kind at a dinner-party than on any other occasion.

On sitting down to dinner, unfold your napkin and place it across your knees. If your roll or piece of bread is on your napkin, place it on the table to the *left* of your plate. At a formal dinner, a *menu* or bill of fare, giving a catalogue of the various dishes in the order in which they are served, is placed in front of each guest or is to be found on the table within reach, so that the guests can consult it and mentally make choice of the dishes they intend to partake of. Make up your mind beforehand as to what you intend to eat or drink, so that there may be no hesitation when the servants bring round the dishes.

When the servant brings you the soup, use the (table) spoon which you will find placed lengthwise behind your plate. In raising the spoon to the lips, place the fingers under the handle, the thumb at the top, and drink the soup noiselessly from the *side* of the spoon; do not put it straight into your mouth. In taking your soup, it is permissible to tilt your plate slightly; but if you do so, tilt it *from* you and not towards you.

Break your bread with your fingers and do not cut or bite it. In eating fish, use the silver fish knives and forks that you will find on either side of your plate. If there are none provided, use *two* forks; never a knife or a spoon. The old custom, in eating fish, of employing a large piece of bread to assist the single fork, is quite obsolete now-a-days.

In helping yourself to salt, use the salt spoon, never your own knife. If the salt spoon should by any chance be missing (as sometimes happens at public tables), use the handle end of your fork or dessert spoon. Some *entrées* or side-dishes require a knife to eat them with; but where you can manage without a knife, do so, and use only a fork.

Peas must always be eaten with a fork, never with a knife or a spoon, though the knife may be used to push them on to the fork.

With joints, venison, poultry, game, &c., knives must of course be used, but on no account put a knife into or up to the mouth, whatever you are eating.

Never take the bone of a chicken or other bird up in your fingers and apply it to your mouth. The meat must be *cut* off the bone, and then eaten with a fork.

Many *sikkins* can be eaten with a fork alone. Do not use a knife, unless you find it necessary, as for snipe or quail.

Most puddings require only a fork; if they are too light (as custards) to be so eaten, supplement your fork with a dessert spoon, but never think of using a knife.

In eating cheese, use a knife only, not a fork. Cut the cheese into small pieces and place each morsel, as required, upon little pieces of (buttered) bread or biscuit. The two should be held in the finger and thumb of the left hand, and so conveyed to the mouth.

Ice-pudding or ices are eaten with a small spoon.

Whenever forks can be used, it is more in accordance with good manners to use them than to use spoons. Knives are used only with an eatable that requires to be *cut.* In eating anything with a fork alone, the fork must be held in the right hand.

Salads (and mayonnaise) are eaten with both knife and fork.

In eating cooked stone-fruit, the best way is first to separate the stones from the fruit with your fork and spoon, and place them on the edge of your plate; you can then eat the fruit without having subsequently to eject the stone from your mouth. After you have finished, remove the stones from the edge to the middle part of your plate; and do the same with any remnants left upon the plate after you have finished a dish.

Asparagus is held between the fingers, dipped into the sauce, and so raised to the mouth and eaten.

When the cheese-plates are removed, the servant will bring you a dessert-plate covered with a doily (or small napkin), upon which rests an ice-plate, and upon that a finger-glass. Remove the finger-glass and the doily, and place them towards your left hand. The servant will then hand round the ice-pudding. Sometimes, however, portions of ice-pudding are served out to the guests; and this is the better plan, because ice-pudding is rather an awkward dish for a guest to deal with.

Do not help yourself to dessert. The servants will take the dishes off the table and hand them round to the guests.

In using your finger-glass, dip the ends of your fingers in the water and touch your mouth slightly with them, and then wipe both with your napkin.

Wine, generally sherry [1] and claret, is passed round the table from right to left during dessert for each guest to take what he pleases. If the lady sitting on your left

---

[1] We may speak of "port wine" but of "sherry wine" never. Say "sherry" (and "claret," and "hock") without adding "wine."

wishes for a glass of wine, she would not help herself, but it would be your duty to pour it out for her.

As soon as the ladies rise to withdraw, the gentlemen rise at the same time, and pushing back their chairs, make room for the ladies to pass; they stand by their chairs until all the ladies have left the room, when they resume their seats. The gentleman nearest the door draws the ***purdah*** aside for the ladies to pass out. On rising, remove your napkin from your knees and place it on the left side of your plate, but without folding it.

A toothpick may be used, if necessary, after the departure of the ladies; but it must never be produced in their presence. Never resort to the perceptible assistance of the tongue in freeing the mouth or teeth from food, or use your finger for the purpose.

When the ladies have left, the gentlemen close up at the table near their host, or if one gentleman wishes to talk to another on the other side of the table, he may go round and take a seat besides him. Wine is passed round, followed by cigars (or cigarettes) and coffee.

In taking tea or coffee, do not suck or gulp it down, but sip it noiselessly. The spoon is to be used only to stir it, or to remove any floating matter from the cup to the saucer. Never pour the tea or coffee from the cup into the saucer; if it is too hot to drink, wait for it to cool. Any tea or coffee that may have fallen into the saucer is to be left where it is, and is not to be drunk. Leave the spoon in the saucer and not in the cup, and do not drain the contents to the last dregs.

After the lapse of from ten minutes to half an hour, the host will take the opportunity of a lull in the conversation to propose an adjournment to the drawing-room. The gentleman of highest rank leaves the dining-room first, the host following last.

In stepping with other gentlemen through a doorway, do not push yourself forward and try to get in front of others; but, at the same time, if another makes way for you, and desires you to pass out before him, do not insist upon drawing back, and thus cause delay and obstruction, but bow and obey. Remember that compliance with, and deference to, the wishes of others is the finest breeding.

On reaching the drawing-room, the gentlemen disperse themselves among the ladies and converse in groups or *tête-à-tête* couples. Generally, some of the guests will play or sing; and while a song is being sung, it is good manners to suspend your conversation and listen to it. To chatter during a song is very impolite, especially if the singer is a lady. Guests will commonly talk when only an instrumental performance is going on; but if you talk, it should be in a subdued tone; it is more polite to remain silent.

As during calls (see p. 23), conversation at and after dinner should be on general topics. Avoid dashing into the conversation at the dinner-table; wait for an opportunity, and then say what you have to say. Always *look* at the person who addresses you and with whom you are talking.

Do not try to enter into a conversation with some one on the opposite side of the table; your duty is to talk to, and endeavour to entertain, those sitting next to you.

Remember that it is very bad taste to talk *across* a person, *i. e.*, to converse with a lady or gentleman with whom you are acquainted sitting on the other side of a lady or gentleman with whom you are not acquainted.

In conversing with people, do not "talk shop:" *i. e.*, if you are a barrister, do not talk about law; or if you are a student, do not talk about your studies. Adapt your conversation as far as possible to your company; and talk rather about subjects that will interest them than about those that interest yourself.

If anyone tells a story or relates an incident with which you are already familiar, do not say "I have heard that before," but listen politely.

Do not interlard your remarks with poetical or other quotations. To do so looks as if you wanted to display your knowledge of the authors you quote; at best, it sounds pedantic in general society.

Do not correct any slight inaccuracies that you may detect in the statements of others. It is polite to let them pass.

If you do not catch a remark that is made to you, do not say "What?" or "What did you say?", but say, "I beg your pardon"

At a dinner-party do not say anything either in praise or blame of the dishes. Do not speak of viands as unwholesome, or say in refusing a dish that "you are afraid of it," or that "it will disagree with you." At table all allusions to dyspepsia, indigestion, &c., are unpleasant and to be avoided.

The usual hour for leaving the house after a dinner-party is from half-past ten to eleven o'clock. The lady of highest rank is the first to take leave; and you should wait, before withdrawing, for her to give the signal. The other guests will rise for departure at the same time, and the party breaks up. Go up to your hostess (and host) and shake hands with her and bid her good-night. It is enough to say "Good-night,[1] Mrs. (*or* Mr.) Jones." Do not express any thanks for her hospitality; that is acknowledged by a subsequent call (see p. 14).

Do not walk round the room making ceremonious adieux to all assembled. Shake hands with a friend, if near you; but for ordinary acquaintances, a civil bow (with or without the words "Good-night"), as you pass them on your way out of the room, is sufficient.

The host should first conduct the lady of highest rank from the drawing-room to her carriage, and then others as he has the opportunity.

Do not offer any gratuities to the servants of the house either at your arrival or departure.

Spirits and soda-water with cigars are generally offered to gentlemen-guests in the hall or dining-room below, on leaving; or, if only gentlemen are present at the party, the bottles and glasses, &c., may be brought upstairs, and cigars are smoked in the verandah.

---

[1] Remember that "Good-night" is only a *parting* salutation. "Good evening" should be said at meeting.

CHAPTER V.

GARDEN-PARTIES—WALKING AND DRIVING.

Garden-parties.—The more formal style of invitation to a garden party is printed in black on large-sized cards, thus :—

NAWAB ABDUL RAHMAN[1]
requests the pleasure of
MR. AND MRS. G. ROBINSON'S
company at a Garden Party
on Tuesday, December 20th, from 4 to 7 p.m.

Chatta Munzil;
Nov. 30, 1886.

R. S. V. P.[2]

All this is printed except the name of the guest or guests.

At Home cards, of a smaller size, are used for the less formal style of invitation, the name of the guest being written at the top of the card, thus :—

MR. J. H. HENDERSON.
BABU NILMANI BANERJI
At Home,
Tuesday, December 20th,
4 to 7 p.m.

151, Park Street;
Dec. 3, 1886.

Garden Party.

---

[1] Among Europeans such invitations are issued in the name of the lady. If, therefore, the Indian host has a wife who mixes in English society, her name, instead of her husband's, should figure on the card of invitation.

[2] Or these letters (explained on p. 28) may be better omitted. Answers are seldom required to invitations of this kind.

Invitations should be sent out from three weeks to a fortnight beforehand, and, when *R. S. V. P.* is put on the card, should be answered immediately.

Sometimes an afternoon dance takes place at a garden party, in which case, the word "Dancing" should be written or printed below "Garden Party" on the card of invitation.

The usual way of receiving guests at a garden party is for the host and hostess, or the hostess only, to stand on the lawn, not far from the entrance to the grounds, a *dhurri* or carpet being generally spread on the grass for her to stand on.

Each guest, on arriving, bows to, or shakes hands with, the hostess (and host), and then passes on and mixes with the company present. There is no need to be punctual at a garden party; you may arrive an hour late, if you like; but if you are late, you may probably not find your hostess standing ready to receive you, and you will have to seek her out among the company, if you wish to pay your respects to her.

At Government House Garden-parties, Her Excellency waits under a *shamiana* near the entrance to receive her guests, who are introduced to her by the Aidé-de-camp in waiting. On being introduced, make a polite bow or *salaam*, and pass on. Do not offer to shake hands or enter into conversation; but leave it to her to do so if she thinks proper. It is advisable to arrive at the grounds in good time, so as not to omit the introduction to Her Excellency.

At garden-parties, people usually walk about the grounds and converse together, or play at some out-door game, as lawn-tennis or badminton. The grounds are often illuminated at dusk with Chinese lanterns, &c., and fireworks or fire-balloons are sometimes provided for the amusement of the guests. There is no ceremony about a garden party, and no order of precedence is observed.

Light refreshments (such as tea and coffee, ices, champagne or claret cup, thin slices of bread and butter, biscuits, cake, and sweetmeats) are provided on tables under a *shamiana*, where chairs are also placed, so that the ladies can sit down and take refreshments, while the gentlemen attend to their wants.

Remember not to partake too freely of the refreshments supplied at a garden party or other public gathering. They are meant to 'refresh' you, not to provide you with a meal. Eat and drink, therefore, slowly and sparingly, and do not make pickings from various dishes or stuff your children with sweetmeats. Avoid fingering viands unless you mean to eat them, and never think of putting any into your pockets.

If dancing is in the programme, it may take place in a *shamiana* specially arranged for it; (but, for a dance. people generally adjourn to the house as it grows dusk, where a room or a suite of rooms has been previously set in order for dancing, which goes on till the close of the proceedings.)

If you remain till the break-up of the party, you should shake hands with, and bid good evening to, your hostess (and host); but if you leave earlier, it is not etiquette to do so.

If you have adopted European clothes, morning dress (as described on p. 20) should be worn at a garden party ; if you wear the Indian dress, the costume described on pp. 19, 20 should be worn. If the weather is cold and you find a shawl necessary, let it be one of elegant material, but quiet in colour. Do not swathe your neck in a gaudy woollen comforter ; if you have a sorethroat or a severe cold, so that you cannot do without it, it is better to stay at home. Gloves are unnecessary. A polished walking-cane (not a rough stick) may be carried ; but do not take with you a cotton sunumbrella ; if you wish to carry an umbrella, it should be a black silk one. Be careful to wear *black* leather shoes or boots, either of patent leather or well polished with blacking ; brown leather or canvas shoes are inadmissible.

As regards general demeanour at garden-parties, places of public promenade or resort, &c.,—if you wear European dress and meet a lady of your acquaintance who bows to you, you should salute her in return by taking off your hat with a slight bow of the head, but without bending your body. Raise your hat with your right hand if the lady is passing you on your left ; with your left hand, if she is passing you on your right ; the hat is always to be taken off on the side away from her. It is the English custom for the lady to bow first ; so that you would not bow to a lady till she had bowed to you, when you should be ready at once to return her salute. If a lady have offended you, and you do not wish to acknowledge her acquaintance, you are still bound to return her bow, though you may do so in a cold and distant manner. In the case of a lady, a direct "cut" from a gentleman is inadmissible.

If the person whom you wish to salute is a gentleman, you would not, as a rule, lift your hat; a nod of the head, or a *salaam*, is sufficient. But if the gentleman you salute is of high dignity or if you wish to show special respect to him, you should raise your hat from your head instead of giving the ordinary nod. European gentlemen always raise their hats to the Viceroy, or a Governor, or a Lieutenant-Governor, or the Head of an Administration; and students at the English Universities always lift their hats to the tutors or other dons of their colleges.

European gentlemen, on being introduced to each other, if the introduction takes place out of doors, always raise their hats in bowing to each other.

If you wear the Indian dress, since the turban is not removed, a polite *salaam* is the appropriate form of salutation, both in the case of a lady and a gentleman.

If you meet a gentleman of your acquaintance, who is walking with a lady (or ladies) whom you do not know, instead of merely nodding, you would raise your hat (if you wore one) to the gentleman, whoever he was, as a mark of respect to the lady who accompanied him; and he, in return, would raise his hat to you. Such a bow would not be looked upon as a bow to the lady, nor would she acknowledge it; and it would not constitute an acquaintance afterwards between you and the lady.

Again, on meeting a gentleman that you know walking with a lady with whom you are unacquainted, it is not etiquette to stop and try to shake hands with or speak to him (unless he makes the first move, when he would probably introduce you to the lady); you should merely bow as prescribed above, and pass on.

At a garden party, promenade, or reception, if you see an English gentleman with whom you are acquainted, do not at once go up to him and offer to shake hands with him. It is better, under ordinary circumstances, to remain where you are, or walk on, and when you catch his eye, to bow or *salaam* to him. English gentlemen are not much given to shaking hands with one another. If the gentleman is of higher position than yourself, and he stops to greet you, do not be the first to hold out your hand to shake hands with him; wait till he holds out his hand to you.

In going up to any one to shake hands, do not walk several yards with extended hand, but put out your hand when you are quite close to the person you greet.

Walking and Driving.—When you are out walking, do not swing your stick or umbrella about, or stand with it placed horizontally under your arm; by doing so you will be in danger of giving an unintentional blow to a passer-by.

Do not sway your arms violently to and fro, or let them dangle limply by your side: the arms should move naturally with the motion of the body.

If you are passing ladies at a place of public promenade, and the path is crowded, you should not march straight ahead, but should politely make way for the ladies by stepping aside.

The general rule of the *pathway* is that passers-by should take their right hand side, so that those who meet them pass them on their left. The English rule of the *road* is the reverse of this, since riders and drivers, in passing each other from opposite directions, take the left hand side of the road. If, in riding or driving, you want to pass another rider or driver going in the same direction as yourself, you should pass him on his right hand side.

If you are taking ladies or gentlemen with you for a drive in your carriage, since they are your guests, politeness requires that you should let them sit with their faces to the horses. If more than two ladies or gentlemen are driving with you, the two that are of the higher rank would occupy the better seat.

When gentlemen and ladies are driving together, gentlemen should always step out of a carriage first, whether they intend to resume their seats or not, so that they may be ready to help the ladies to alight. They should also help them to get into the carriage.

When there is more than one lady present, if the additional lady is not a member of his family, the gentleman would in most cases sit with his back to the horses: otherwise, he would sit by the lady's side.

When a gentleman goes out riding with a lady, he should ride on her "off" or right hand side. Similarly, when a gentleman and a lady walk out together, the lady would usually walk on his left hand side or take his left arm, so that the gentleman may have his right arm disengaged to take off his hat to any lady of his acquaintance he may meet. It is, however, unusual for a lady to take a gentleman's arm when walking abroad, unless she is weak or tired. But if they are walking along a street, the gentleman would give the lady the side of the pathway next to the houses, and himself take the side next the road. If you are in the company of ladies, when there are lofty steps to be mounted, it is etiquette for you to lead the way up the steps and for the ladies to follow. To insist upon the ladies mounting before you, would be a mistaken piece of politeness. But it is quite etiquette for you to offer your arm to a lady to help her in making the ascent.

Should you, whilst walking with a friend, whether Indian or European, meet a European acquaintance, do not introduce them to each other, unless you have reason to believe that such an introduction would be agreeable to both parties. If, however, you stop and speak to the acquaintance, you place your friend in an awkward position unless you introduce him; it is better, therefore, in such a case, merely to bow and pass on.

Should accidental circumstances, at any time, bring you into communication with a lady who is a stranger to you (as, for instance, if she should drop anything, and you politely pick it up for her)—on such an occasion, you should raise your hat, if you wear one, and make a bow, or, if you wear the Indian costume, you should make a courteous *salaam*.

CHAPTER VI.

LEVÉES, DURBARS, RECEPTIONS, VISITS.

Levées.—The announcement of a Levée to be held at Government House is published in the newspapers with instructions as to the forms to be observed by those who wish to attend. The date is given on or before which the cards of such persons must be sent in an envelope addressed to "The Aide-de-camp in waiting, Government House." It is sufficient for each person to send one card, with his name printed or legibly written thereon along with his designation, and with the word "Levée" written in the upper left-hand corner. The address should be placed in the lower left-hand corner. The word "Levée" may also be written in the upper left-hand corner of the envelope.

A gentleman going to a Levée should carry two similar cards with him, one to be given to the Government House attendant at the foot of the staircase, and the other to be handed to the Aide-de-camp in waiting in the Throne Room.

A gentleman who, being socially eligible, has not already been presented at the English Court or at Government House, must be presented by another gentleman who is on the Government House List. The gentleman so presented should write "To be presented by ———" (giving the name of his presenter) in the upper left-hand corner of the card sent to the Aide-de-camp in waiting.

European or Indian full or evening dress (as described on pp. 19, 20) must invariably be worn at a Levée; and Indian gentlemen should divest themselves of wrappings immediately after entering Government House. In Calcutta, a place for their deposit is provided in the great hall directly opposite the main entrance, where they are usually ticketed with a number, and a counterfoil bearing the same number is given to the wearer, so that there need be no fear of the loss of the article. Do not go into the presence of the Viceroy (or Governor) with a shawl tied round your shoulders, or with your throat enveloped in a woollen comforter.

After depositing your outer wrappings you will join the stream of arrivals[1] and gradually make your way from barrier to barrier until you reach the Throne Room. The arrangements are, or should be, such as to prevent any crowding, so that jostling and elbowing are avoided.

On arriving at the Throne Room, the group of gentlemen break up into single file and walk slowly forward past the throne where the Viceroy (or Governor) stands to acknowledge their salutes. Take your place in the file and advance leisurely with your card ready in your hand to be given to the Aide-de-camp in waiting. He will take it from you and hand it on to the Military Secretary, who will announce your name just before you arrive opposite the Viceroy.

---

[1] Unless you have *Private Entrée;* in which case you will enter Government House by another door, and make your bow to the Viceroy before the admission of the general public.

Upon your name being announced, you should take a step forward, and facing round to the Viceroy at a respectful distance, make an inclination of the body, accompanied, if you are in Indian costume, by a *salaam*. You will then retire by an exit on the opposite side of the room to that by which you entered. As you leave the immediate presence of the Viceroy, avoid directly turning your back upon him by taking a few steps in a sideways direction.

On leaving the Throne Room, you are at liberty to stay a while in the entrance hall and converse with your friends. But you should be ready to depart as soon as your carriage arrives, since carriages are not permitted to wait at the door for their occupants, who must be on the look-out, so as to step into them at once.

Durbars.—Durbars are often held for the presentation of *khilluts* and *sunnuds* to Indian gentlemen on whom titles have been conferred by Government, by the Viceroy or the Chief Civil Officer of the Province, or by the Commissioner of the Division, or the Collector at the Sudder Station.

Indian officers of rank and the Indian gentry of the neighbourhood are invited to be present on these occasions, who should appear in full dress (see pp. 19, 20).

All Indian gentlemen present, including the recipients of *khilluts*, if they wear shoes of Indian fashion, must take them off before entering the Durbar Hall. This regulation does not, of course, apply to boots or shoes of European fashion.

The Indian gentry have their chairs on the right hand

side of the Presiding Officer's chair, according to their rank. On the left are placed chairs for all public functionaries and officers, who are seated according to their rank, &c.

It is important to arrive in good time at a Durbar, as the audience are expected to be assembled and seated before the arrival of the Presiding Officer.

On the arrival of the recipient of the *khillut*, the Chief Secretary or other Officer leads him up to the Presiding Officer's chair. As soon as he reaches it, the whole audience show their respect by rising from their chairs.

The recipient of the *khillut* is then conducted to an adjoining room, where he is robed with the different *parchas* of the *khillut*, except the pearl necklace. He is then brought back into the Durbar Hall, and stands in front of the Presiding Officer, who rises (along with the whole audience) and ties the pearl necklace round the recipient's neck.

The *sunnud* conferring the title is then read by the Secretary of the Political Department, or sometimes a vernacular translation is read by some high Indian officer selected for the purpose, and the recipient, after presenting the usual *nuzzuranah* of gold mohurs, resumes his seat.

After a short pause, the Presiding Officer orders *attar* and *pan* to be brought, and, standing up, serves them out first to the recipient of the *khillut*, and then to all the Indian gentlemen of high rank present, who are summoned before the Presiding Officer for the purpose. Some official subordinate to the Presiding Officer serves them out to the rest of the Indian gentlemen present. The Durbar then closes, and the audience take their leave.

Receptions, Visits.—When a Governor, Lieutenant-Governor, &c., visits a District, the local officer arranges beforehand a time on certain days during which the former will receive any Indian or other gentlemen who may desire an interview; and those wishing to see him should call and send in their cards at the time fixed. Only Rajahs, Nawabs, and other specially distinguished persons should apply by letter for an interview; and they should write to the Private Secretary, asking when the Lieutenant-Governor, &c., will be willing to see them. In case of a Commissioner visiting a District, those who are desirous of an interview with him, should write to the Magistrate and Collector of the District to that effect.

On entering the presence of the Lieutenant-Governor, &c., the Indian visitor should make a polite bow and *salaam*, but should not offer to shake hands, unless his host holds out his hand for that purpose. He should also remain standing until he is invited to take a seat.

During the interview, the general rules of behaviour given under *Calls* (pp. 18, 19) should be followed. As soon as the preliminary expressions of welcome and politeness are over, and the host has finished anything he may have had to say, the visitor should come *at once* to the object of his interview. He should not carry on a long conversation on miscellaneous subjects, and then, when it is time to take his leave, bring forward the real object of his visit. He should bear in mind that the time of a Lieutenant-Governor or a Commissioner, especially when on tour, is much occupied, and is too valuable to be expended in chatting about general topics. He should, therefore, get through the object of his visit *as quickly as possible*, and then, as the conversation flags, and it is clear that he is expected to retire, he should ask if he may take leave. On retiring, the Indian visitor should bow and *salaam* as on entering; or he may shake hands with his host, should the latter offer to do so.

CHAPTER VII.

WEDDINGS.

INVITATIONS to a wedding are issued about three weeks or a fortnight before the event; and it is usual now-a-days for friends who are invited to send the bride or bridegroom a present.

If, however, the invitation is sent to you only a day or two before the wedding, you will hardly be expected to send a present.

Wedding presents may be sent at any time during the interval between your receipt of the invitation and the day fixed for the marriage—one time is as correct as another.

Should the marriage engagement be broken off during this interval, all wedding presents are returned at once to the donors.

Before sending a present, write "With Mr. (*or* Babu, &c.) ———'s best wishes" on a card or a neat slip of paper, and attach it to the present. This is sufficient; no letter addressed to the recipient need accompany the present. You will receive in return a note of acknowledgment from the recipient.

Wedding presents are very various. Such as the following are generally acceptable:—Some elegant article of furniture, dessert services, breakfast or tea and coffee sets, clocks, lamps, screens, photograph albums, writing-cases, dressing-cases, vases, salvers, breakfast cruets, fish-knives and forks, a set of silver salt-cellars, &c.

Perhaps, however, the best present for an Indian gentleman to make is some elegant piece of jewellery, as a bracelet or ring.

In making presents generally, remember that, as a rule, a gift should be precious for something better than its price, as for its being something unique or antique, or for the thoughtfulness shown by the giver. Bouquets to ladies, game (as snipe, teal, &c.) to gentlemen, are often elegant and acceptable presents. Do not give expecting a return, and never allude to your present. When you give anything, do not either undervalue the gift or make a great deal of it; make your present quietly and gracefully, without grudging and without display.

Invitations are specially printed for the occasion in silver on white paper with a silver border, and are enclosed in envelopes also having a silver border.

The following is the correct form :—

MR. AND MRS. ROBINSON
request the pleasure of
BABU (*or* MR.) SURENDRA NATH GHOSE'S
company at St. Paul's Church, on Monday, December 3rd, at 4-30 p.m., on the occasion of the marriage of their daughter with Mr. J. H. Jones, and afterwards at 103, Chowringhee.

R. S. V. P.[1]

---

[1] **Sometimes these letters (see p. 28) are omitted; in which case, of course, no answer is necessary.**

On receiving such an invitation, you should answer it at once, in case of acceptance, thus:—

Babu (*or* Mr.) Surendra Nath Ghose has much pleasure in accepting Mr. and Mrs. Robinson's kind invitation to their daughter's wedding, on Monday, December 3rd.

154, Wellesley Street;
Nov. 12, 1887.

In case of refusal, thus:—

Babu (*or* Mr.) Surendra Nath Ghose much regrets that he is unable to accept &c.

If there is anything to prevent your attendance at the church, but you can be present at the house afterwards, you should still accept the invitation in the form given above. There is no necessity for you to mention your inability to attend at the church.

If you go to the church, you should be punctual, so as to make sure of arriving *before* the bride; to arrive after her is a breach of etiquette.

On arriving, take your seat in a pew, but avoid the pews immediately in front, since these are generally occupied by the bride's or the bridegroom's relatives.

The bride, on arriving, walks up the aisle of the church towards the altar, escorted by her father (or other near relative or friend), followed by the bridesmaids, walking two and two, and, after them, by her mother, leaning on the arm of some near relation or friend.

As the bridal procession advances up the aisle, it is usual for those present to stand up.

As soon as the marriage service is over, the bride and bridegroom, preceded by the officiating clergyman, and followed by the bridesmaids, &c., pass in procession down the aisle to the vestry for the purpose of signing the marriage register.

The guests present rise as the procession passes, and afterwards sit or stand about the aisle or portico, waiting for the re-appearance of the bride and bridegroom from the vestry.

Sometimes, during the interval, "wedding favours" (rosettes of white satin ribbon) are distributed by the bridesmaids among the guests; these "favours" are pinned on to the gentlemen's coats in front near the button hole.

The bride and bridegroom are the first to drive away from the church; after them, the bride's mother with other near relatives. As soon as these are gone, the guests are at liberty to depart, in any order, for the house of the bride's father or the one at which she has been staying. They must not leave before; otherwise, when they reached the house, there would be no one to receive them.

On arriving at the house, walk upstairs to the drawing-room, where, just inside the door, you will find the bride and bridegroom standing to receive the congratulations of the guests. Shake hands with both and say, "Accept my sincere congratulations," or some similar expression, and then pass on, so as to make room for other guests to offer theirs.

You should then pay your respects to the lady of the house (unless you have met her before), making some pleasant allusion to the wedding, such as that you thought it a pretty sight, or that it went off very well. If she is the mother of the bride, it is not etiquette to "congratulate" her upon her daughter's marriage; if you desire to say anything on that point, you ought rather to condole with her on the loss of her daughter. But some general remark of an agreeable nature will be sufficient.

You can then mix with the other guests and join in the general conversation.

The wedding presents are usually displayed on a table (or tables) for the inspection of the guests, who walk round and examine them. This gives the guests something to look at and to talk about.

In an adjoining room, or in the verandah, light refreshments with champagne and pieces of the wedding cake are served out to the guests, who partake of them as they feel inclined. There is no formal drinking of the health of the bride and bridegroom, and there are usually no speeches.

The bride then leaves the company to change her wedding for her travelling dress, and the guests await her re-appearance in readiness to bid her adieu.

Rice, and sometimes, slippers are thrown after the newly-married couple by the guests; the latter, after they have entered the carriage.

Soon after, the party breaks up, and the guests take their leave, in any order, of their host and hostess, and drive away.

CHAPTER VIII.

RAILWAY AND STEAM-BOAT TRAVELLING; DAK BUNGALOWS, HOTELS.

Railway Travelling.—In travelling by railway, courtesy and good manners are very important, both for your own comfort and for that of your fellow-passengers.

Do not attempt to contravene the rules and regulations or bylaws of the railway line upon which you travel. They are made for the general interests of the passengers and the traffic, and you have no right to transgress them for your own private convenience. You are also bound to follow the directions of the responsible officials of the line, such as the guard of the train or the station-master. You are at liberty to do so under protest, if you consider their action improper, and to report their conduct to their superiors; but you must submit to their ruling for the time being, and not enter into an altercation with them in public. All public brawls and contentions are a violation of the quiet dignity and self-respect which mark the gentleman.

Some railway lines provide separate carriages for Indian and for European passengers—a plan which has much to recommend it. On lines where no such distinction is made, Indians and Europeans, both ladies and gentlemen, often travel together in the same carriages, and mutual courtesy is necessary, the more because Indians generally differ in their habits and tastes from Europeans.

European gentlemen seldom eat in railway carriages; meals are provided for them at certain fixed stations along the line. They do, however, usually smoke while they are travelling; but, if they smoke in a railway carriage in which an Indian gentleman is present, they are bound first to ask his permission.

Indian gentlemen are fond of chewing *pan* or of smoking the *hookah* while on a journey. But if a European gentleman is present in the carriage, you should try to abstain, as both practices are likely to be distasteful to him. But in any case, before chewing or smoking, you should always politely ask your fellow-passenger whether he has any objection.

Indian gentlemen, again, seldom sleep, or try to sleep, right through the night, at any rate when they are travelling by railway. They like to get up in the middle of the night to chew and smoke, and have a chat with their Indian fellow-passengers. To European travellers in the same carriage, this practice is very unpleasant: their sleep is broken by the noise, and the smell of the *pan* and of the tobacco-fumes is apt to be even more distasteful to them than by day, since the carriage is generally more closed up from the outer air during the night. Endeavour, therefore, to consult the feelings of your European fellow-travellers by not getting up at night to smoke, or chew, or talk. If you wish to sit up for a time, do so quietly, so as to avoid disturbing them.

Try to avoid bringing country sweetmeats, &c., with

you into the carriage, when you are travelling with Europeans. Indian passenger trains have fixed halting-stations, where you can leave the carriage and take any food that you require, and where, too, you can indulge in *pan* and the *hookah*, if you desire to do so. It is best, therefore, to take refreshments at these halting-stations, so as to avoid bringing them into the carriage. If, however, circumstances should at any time require you to do so, eat them at once (such light refreshments can be obtained on the platform of most stations that your train passes), and do not lay in a stock of sweetmeats, and leave them lying about on the carriage-seat, to the annoyance of your fellow-passengers.

Unless you are travelling in a compartment reserved for Indian passengers, never remove all the clothing from the upper part of your person and appear in the scanty attire of the home circle. If the weather is warm, you are at liberty to take off the *choga* or any outer garment; but do not bare your arms and shoulders and reduce your clothing to a mere *dhoti*. This rule of etiquette is, of course, specially to be observed when there are ladies present with you in the carriage. Let your *dhoti* (if you wear one) be of sufficient length, and do not allow it to become disarranged.

Those passengers whose seats are next the windows of a railway carriage, must always have their wishes consulted as to the opening or shutting of the windows, since they are most exposed to draught or sun. If, therefore, you desire to have a window opened or shut, you should first politely ask such passengers whether they have any objection.

Steam-boat Travelling.—In travelling by steamer on Indian rivers, the same general rules of courtesy should be observed. Do not smoke the *hookah* or chew *pan* anywhere on board the vessel where the smell is likely to be unpleasant to your European fellow-passengers. You can easily find a place where you can go apart and smoke or chew without annoyance to others. You should be specially careful on these points if there are ladies on board. Thus, it is better not to indulge in either practice in your cabin; steamer cabins are open to one another at the top for the purpose of ventilation, so that a smell emanating from one cabin circulates through all the rest. Do not, again, appear with bared arms and shoulders in the presence or neighbourhood of Europeans; reserve such "undress" for your cabin or for those parts of the ship that are not frequented by them. Also, be careful here as in railway travelling as to the length and arrangement of your *dhoti* (see pp. 11, 12).

If you take with you on board a quantity of country sweetmeats, &c., for consumption during the voyage, keep them in your cabin; do not let them lie about on your seat on deck or on the public table. Anything you want to eat between meals, it is best to eat in private.

If the weather is very hot, and you, along with the other passengers, sleep on deck in the open, follow the same rules of behaviour as in the case of travelling by rail (see p. 76).

Do not tease the captain or officers of the steamer with unnecessary inquiries or petty complaints. Avoid all fussiness or readiness to take offence; and, as in the case of travelling by railway, be careful to respect all the rules or regulations of the ship, and never enter into a public quarrel with any of the authorities on board.

Dâk Bungalows, Hotels.—Sometimes, in the course of a journey, you may put up at a dâk bungalow or an hotel, where Europeans are also staying. At such places you will almost always find a printed or written list of rules or regulations to guide the behaviour of visitors, posted up where it can be seen by all. There may also be "Notices," &c., put up on the walls of the public rooms. On arriving at the dâk bungalow or the hotel, you should carefully read such rules or notices, unless you are previously acquainted with them, and should then be careful not to infringe them. They are designed for the general comfort of all the guests, and should, therefore, be strictly and unselfishly observed by everyone.

Be gentle and courteous in your treatment of the hotel or dâk bungalow servants, and do not unnecessarily find fault with them. Do not shout at them, or give your orders in a loud voice to the disturbance of other visitors.

If you have adopted English habits, and take your meals at the public table, follow, generally, the rules of behaviour given in the chapter on "Dinner-parties." Since, however, you are nobody's guest, and pay for all that is supplied you, a greater laxity is allowable in some matters. Thus, as soon as the bell or gong has sounded, you are at liberty to take your seat at table and begin the meal without waiting for others; and, similarly, you may leave the table as soon as you have finished eating. If you do not like a dish to which you have helped yourself, you may send it away and ask for another. At dâk bungalows and generally at hotels, there is no rule by which seats at table are set apart for visitors ; those visitors, however, who have been staying for some time at an hotel, usually prefer to retain the seats that they have previously occupied, and to which they have become accustomed. Do not, therefore, on entering the dining-room, seat yourself at once in any vacant chair, but wait for the *khansamah* or other attendant to show you a seat ; and this seat you will, as a rule, occupy during the remainder of your stay. Sometimes, at public tables, you will find chairs tilted forwards against the table ; this denotes that the seats are taken, though the occupants have not yet arrived ; and you are bound to leave such chairs as they are, and take another seat.

It is quite etiquette for persons sitting at table in an hotel or a dâk bungalow to enter into conversation with their neighbours without a previous introduction being necessary. If, however, you are seated next to a lady, it will be better for you to wait for her to speak to you first, unless you have some previous acquaintance with her.

CHAPTER IX.

CHURCH-GOING—THEATRES, PUBLIC MEETINGS, &c.

Church-going.—If you attend a service at a church or a chapel, see that you arrive and take your seat before the commencement of the service. If you come in late, you are liable to disturb the rest of the congregation, and show a want of respect for the feelings and devotions of those present. On entering, do not clatter down the aisle or treat the place of worship as if it were a college class-room or mere public hall. Unless you are an habitual attendant and have a seat of your own, it is usual to wait at the entrance for the verger or other person to conduct you to a seat. In many churches, however, the seats are open to all-comers as soon as the hour has struck or the choir and clergy have entered. In the latter case, you must wait with other strangers at the entrance to the nave till the procession of choristers, &c., have passed in, when you are at liberty to enter and take any vacant sitting. But, whatever the custom of the church or the chapel may be, walk in with as little noise as possible, and seat yourself quietly. To loll in your chair, to jog up and down, or to turn round and stare about you, are most of all improper in a place of divine worship. Do not nod or whisper to a friend or exchange glances with him. Never, under any circumstances, chew *pan* or expectorate in a church or a chapel.

If, after you have taken your seat, another person comes to the pew where you are sitting, and wants to pass by you to another chair in the same pew, you should draw back as much as possible and make way for him. If the person is a lady, it is better to rise, so as to give more room for her to pass you.

If you attend church in the company of a lady or ladies, you should precede them in walking down the aisle, and then wait at the pew-door for them to enter the pew first.

During divine service endeavour to follow the motions of the congregation, and stand or sit when they do. Kneeling, being a distinct form of worship, may be dispensed with. No one obliges you to attend church, and if you do so merely out of curiosity, you are bound, out of courtesy to the rest of the congregation, to conform to the outward order and attitude of the service as far as may be.

As you should not enter late, so you should not leave a church or a chapel till the service is finished. Apart from higher considerations, to do so implies that you are tired of the service, and is disrespectful to the officiating clergyman as well as disturbing to the congregation. In an Episcopal church (but never in a Nonconformist chapel), it is sometimes usual for part of the congregation to leave the building before the sermon. This is done during the singing of the hymn that immediately precedes it, and it is improper to go out at any other time while the service is proceeding. On leaving the church, do not stand about in the lobby, and stare at other outgoers, or talk and laugh in loud tones with your friends, but depart as soberly and quietly as you entered.

Theatres, Public Meetings, &c.—If you attend an English theatre, opera-house, or concert-room, or present yourself at any other secular public gathering frequented by

Europeans, it is well, since you are not among your own people, to be careful, and even somewhat ceremonious, in your general behaviour.

If the public entertainment is held in the evening (as is generally the case with Plays, Concerts, &c.), evening dress, whether European or Indian (see p. 27), should be worn. At Public Meetings, however, held in the evening, evening dress is not necessary, though it is quite correct to wear it. At meetings and performances held during the day time, morning dress (see pp. 19, 20) should be worn.

If you have a ticket for a numbered and reserved seat or stall, hand it, on entering, to the official in attendance, who will point you out your chair. You should see that the number upon it is the same as the number on the counterfoil of your ticket; the ticket itself you will have given up at the door. Should you find your seat taken by somebody else, it is better not to deal with the intruder yourself, but to appeal to the official, who is bound to correct the mistake for you.

You will find it the best plan, both for your own comfort and that of others, to be seated in your place before the performance commences. If, however, you happen to arrive late, enter quietly and noiselessly, so as not to disturb those present who wish to listen to the Play or the music or whatever may be going on. If you have to pass others who are already seated, in order to get to your place, show by your demeanour that you wish to incommode them as little as possible. Do not push hurriedly past them, but step carefully along; and if, during the process, you inadvertently tread on any one's toes or otherwise discompose him, be ready to say at once, "I beg your pardon." If those you desire to pass should happen not to notice your arrival, call their attention to the fact by saying "Excuse me," or "Will you kindly allow me to pass?"

If you have a friend seated at a short distance from you, do not talk to him across the intervening members of the audience (see p. 54), but go round and speak to him (if you wish to do so) during an interval or at the close of the performance.

Such an interval (of about ten minutes) is generally provided between the two parts of a Concert, or smaller intervals (*entr'actes*) are allowed between the different Acts of a Play. During these intervals you are at liberty to leave your seat and chat with friends among the audience, or you may go outside and wait there till the performance recommences. But let your exit and entrance be made quietly and without incommoding those of the audience who prefer to remain seated. If your seat is in the centre of a bench or row, so that you have to push past a good many people in order to get out, it is better not to take advantage of every interval in the theatrical performance to go out, since, by frequently passing to and fro, you will be apt to tire the patience of those who have to make way for you. In such a case, and in similar cases, do not insist upon your rights, but politely waive them for the convenience and comfort of others.

During the progress of the performance, especially if it is a musical one, do not converse with a friend, and so disturb others who wish to listen. If you desire to make an occasional remark to him, do so in a low voice. It is true that some European ladies and gentlemen make a practice of chattering noisily at a theatre, or even at a concert, during the progress of the entertainment; but such behaviour is ill-mannered and not to be imitated.

Applause of the performers is usually indicated by clapping the hands, and the audience may show that they wish a piece to be repeated by cries of *Encore!* (which is French for *Again!*). You are, of course, at liberty to join in such demonstrations, but do not be too noisy in making them.

At theatrical performances an opera glass is useful for viewing the actors and the scenery, and is also employed by Europeans to spy out friends among the audience; but since, in most cases, few friends of yours are likely to be present, it will be better for you to keep your opera-glass for its stage use. If you stare about at the audience with it, you may run the risk of being thought rude.

Abstain from chewing *pan* inside the building; and it is advisable not to do so outside during the intervals in the performance, since the smell is retained in the mouth, and is likely to be unpleasant to those sitting near you. English gentlemen often smoke cigarettes outside during the intervals, and you are, of course, at liberty to do the same, if you wish.

After the performance or meeting is over, leave quietly. Avoid jostling or crowding against others in the attempt to get out quickly, and always be ready to make way for ladies who may want to pass you in order to join their friends or to reach their carriages.

CHAPTER X.

HOUSEHOLD APPOINTMENTS.

In furnishing apartments intended for the use of European guests, an Indian gentleman will find it best, if possible, to consult some European friend on the subject. In default of the opportunity for obtaining such advice, a few hints may be given here.

Remember that English taste prefers neatness and genuineness to splendour and gaudiness. In providing the necessary articles of furniture, place use before show; and, in case of ornamental additions, be particular to avoid all tawdriness.

For a dining-room a large table, cane-seated chairs, a side-board (the shelf or shelves above to hold plated ware, &c., and the cupboard below to contain the crockery), and two dinner what-nots (to hold glassware) are all the furniture necessary. Three or four good engravings or oil-paintings may be placed upon the walls, and pairs of horns may be fixed up above the doorways. But there should be only a few ornaments: the general aspect of a dining-room should be severe rather than gay.

In furnishing a drawing-room, one or two (or more, according to the size of the apartment) small tables,[1] which may be covered with embroidered cloths, should be placed conveniently, here and there, about the room. A sofa or settee, covered with silk or velvet,

---

[1] Several small tables look better and are more convenient than a single large one.

with three or four easy-chairs of the same pattern, occupy the centre, and half-a-dozen light fancy-chairs may be set about near the tables or by the walls, which should be painted in some neutral tint with a quiet (not flaring) design. Carved what-nots may be placed by the walls and at the corners of the room, for the reception of well-bound books and ornamental items, such as vases, bric-a-brac, china, &c. A good piano with music-stand and music-stool should also be provided. One or two *good* water-colours in gilt frames, with some etchings or high-class engravings in ornamental wooden frames, may adorn the walls; to which also a few china or *cloissoné* plates may be fastened, with plush-covered brackets here and there to hold vases, &c. A drawing-room may, and should be, more ornamental than a dining-room; but do not overcrowd the room with a profusion of knicknacks of all sorts, and be very careful that everything is good of its kind. Thus, do not cover the walls of the drawing-room (or of the entrance hall or staircase) with tawdry German coloured prints purchased by the dozen, or with gaudy oleographs; and remember that artificial flowers under glass shades, sewing-machines, &c. are not becoming ornaments for drawing-room tables.

A bed-room, which should have a bath-room attached to it, should be furnished with a bedstead (with mattress, two pillows, two sheets and a blanket or *resai*), an *almirah* and chest of drawers, a dressing-table with looking-glass, a washhand-stand, a couch, and three or four chairs. A good picture or two are not out of place on the walls, but are not necessary.

CHAPTER. XI.

LETTERS, APPLICATIONS, MEMORIALS, PETITIONS, TESTIMONIALS, ADDRESSES.

Letters, Applications.—In writing letters in English to English people, adapt your style to the kind of letter you are composing. Thus, if you are addressing a friend, you may adopt an easy colloquial style, as if you were talking to him; if, on the other hand, you are addressing a superior, you should use a more careful and exact style. But, in either case, let your language be simple and direct, and avoid the exaggerated expression of your feelings or flattery of your correspondent. English gentlemen, when writing to one another on ordinary topics, avoid strong displays of emotion and profuse compliments, which, however, may be quite in keeping with oriental taste, and sound appropriate in an oriental language. The great point in ordinary letter-writing is for the writer to understand exactly the meaning he wishes to convey, and to endeavour to express that meaning in the most simple and natural language at his command.

If you possess a crest or a coat of arms, you may have them stamped in gold or in colours, with or without the motto, in the centre near the top of your note-paper; or a monogram may be so placed. Your direction may also be printed or stamped in colours on the right hand side of the note-paper near the top. Such stamping is better done simply and neatly. Try to avoid display in these as in other matters.

Write with black ink rather than with red or violet; and if you require to use sealing-wax, let it be red, unless you are in mourning, when it should be black.

In writing letters containing applications for situations, those circumstances should be mentioned which strengthen the applicant's claim: such as the education he has received, the examinations he has passed, the appointments he has held, together with any special qualifications he may have for the post. Other personal details regarding the applicant's poverty or the large family dependent on him, and appeals to the benevolence of the person addressed, should be sparingly introduced, since they have very little weight in determining the bestowal of an appointment, especially if the post is one in the Public Service.

Write concisely and to the point, and be careful not to omit to date your application.

The candidate's testimonials should accompany his application. They may be printed from the originals, or copies may be sent which should be marked in each case, at the top, "True Copy." The originals should not be sent with the application, though they may be subsequently applied for. Such copies should be fairly and legibly written and on good paper, as well as the application itself; and it should be seen that the copies are accurate reproductions of the originals. Applications and testimonials written in slovenly style and on poor paper are apt to raise a prejudice against the applicant in the mind of the recipient. Similarly, it is important that the application should contain no errors in grammar or spelling, and should be written in good idiomatic English.

Applications for appointments under Government are often incorrectly made by Indian gentlemen direct to the Governor or Lieutenant-Governor or other Head of a Province. Such applications are usually transferred, without comment by their Private Secretary to the Chief Secretary, and are dealt with by him as he thinks fit. Except, therefore, in very special or peculiar circumstances, an Indian gentleman should address his application in the first instance to the Chief Secretary to the Government to which he belongs; and, even so, the applicant must be prepared to receive a reply directing him to address his application to the local authorities for any post for which he may wish to apply.

To make a general application for *any* post under Government is of little or no avail. The applicant should specify the particular appointment or at any rate the kind of appointment for which he is a candidate. Appointments under Government, both in the higher and in the subordinate Services, are now-a-days made on the results of competitive examination, modified to a certain extent by Nomination; but a candidate must not expect to be allowed to forego the examination test and to obtain a post by Nomination, unless he have very special claims to consideration or be placed in very exceptional circumstances.

Shun the writing of anonymous letters. There are

very few cases in which they are justifiable. Such letters are often written to complain of the action or to reveal the real or supposed misdeeds of some subordinate to his official superior; but if the complaint or the misdeed are grounded on fact (of which the writer should make quite sure), the letter containing them must be signed as a guarantee of good faith. Otherwise, such letters can carry no weight, since they are mere irresponsible utterances, and are fitly consigned to the waste-paper basket. If the charges made are true, and you feel that it is your duty to make them, it is equally your duty in the interests of justice to append your signature, in order that your statement may receive due attention from the person addressed.

Similarly, be chary of ventilating your grievances in anonymous letters to the Editor of a newspaper. If you are in Government (or other) service, apply to the Head of your Office for redress. To appeal to the public on your own personal matters in the columns of a newspaper is a breach of official etiquette, and is likely to be of little benefit to yourself. A straightforward representation of your case to your superior will meet with attention if it deserves it.

As regards letters of Introduction, *i.e.*, letters given by you to a friend in order to introduce him to another friend of yours—do not be too ready to write such letters. They should not be lightly given to a mere acquaintance; since, by so doing, you act unfairly towards the friend to whom you write, in introducing to him a person of whom you know but little. Avoid also exaggerating the merits of the person on whose behalf you write the letter. A letter of Introduction should be given *unsealed* to the recipient, who fastens it up before transmitting it to the person to whom it is addressed (see p. 15).

If you receive a long or important letter from any one, which requires consideration on your part, so that there is some delay in replying to it, the proper etiquette is for you to send a brief note at once to the writer, acknowledging receipt of the letter and promising an answer as soon as possible.

The following general hints on letter-writing may be noted.

Avoid the ungrammatical use of the expression *and oblige* as an ending to letters containing a request. The phrase is, at the best, rather a hackneyed one, but it is not incorrect to attach it to the words expressing the request: as, "Please grant me leave *and oblige* Yours obediently," &c.; but it is a blunder in grammar to attach *oblige* in the imperative or the infinitive mood by the conjunction *and* to a verb which is not in either of these moods: as, "I shall be thankful for any assistance *and oblige* Yours obediently," &c.

Beware also of the ungrammatical use of *Yours* for *Your* in the subscription: as, *Yours obedient servant.* The mistake probably arises from a confusion of the two forms, *Yours obediently* and *Your obedient servant.* When, therefore, the noun is expressed, *your* must be used. Observe also that the correct spelling is *yours* not *your's.*

Two different titles, such as *Mr.* (or *The Hon.*) along with *Esq.*, should not be used together. Thus we write

The Hon. J. B. Smith, not *The Hon. J. B. Smith, Esq.*[1]

When *Dear*, *My dear*, are used, *Esq.* and *Hon.* should not be added, nor the capital letters denoting Degrees, &c. Thus we write *Dear Mr. Jones*, but not *Dear Jones, Esq.*, or *Dear Hon. Jones, C.S. I.*

Care should be taken to avoid inappropriate forms of subscription, such as *Yours affectionately* in a business letter or *Your humble servant* in a letter to a friend.

The habit of underlining every word meant to be emphatic should be avoided; it is generally possible to construct a sentence in such a form as to indicate by the position of a word any stress that is to be laid upon it.

The frequent use of parentheses generally causes obscurity.

Abbreviations or contractions, such as *Yrs.* for *Yours*, *tho'* for *though*, imply haste or negligence, and are, therefore, inadmissible except in business letters to or from tradesmen; but in familiar letters, conversational contractions, such as *I'm*, *I'll*, *don't*, *can't*, *won't*, *&c.*, are permissible.

Postscripts seem to indicate thoughtlessness in the writer, and should be avoided in formal correspondence.

Mistakes are often made by Indian gentlemen from the difficulty they have in distinguishing between polite forms of speech which involve a *request* and others that differ but slightly from them, but which really imply a *command*.

Thus, the phrase *I will thank you to send* (often wrongly written "I *shall* thank you to send") is im-

[1] But we write—*The Hon. Mr. Justice Smith, The Right Honourable Sir R. Cross, The Hon. and Rev. B. Jones, General Sir H. Thompson.*

properly used in making a request, since it really implies a command, and is frequently employed to express anger or indignation, as in "I will thank you to mind your own business."

The following are polite forms of *command* :—

(1) Have the goodness to send, *or* Be good enough to send, *or* Be so kind as to send, *or* Oblige me by sending.

(2) Please send *or* Kindly send.

The forms in (2) are less peremptory than those in (1). An authoritative command is implied in the expressions, *You will be good enough to send*, *I will thank you to send* ; while *I shall be obliged if you will send*, *I should be glad if you would send* give the command in a more indirect and courteous form ; and when they are modified by the introduction of the adverbs *much*, *extremely*, *&c.*, (as, *I should be much obliged*, &c.) cannot be said to involve a command at all.

The following are polite forms of *request* :—

(1) Will you kindly send? *or* Will you be kind enough to send? *or* Will you be so kind as to send? *or* Will you have the kindness to send?

(2) Would you kindly send? *or* Would you be kind enough to send? *or* Would you be so kind as to send? *or* Would you have the kindness to send?

The forms in (2) are less direct (since they imply a conditional clause, such as "If I were to ask you"), and, therefore, are more polite than those in (1).

A request may also be implied by the use of the phrases—*I should esteem it a great favour if you would send*, *You would greatly oblige me by sending*, and the like.

A tone of formality and ceremony is imparted to letters by avoiding the use of the first and second persons of pronouns and verbs. Thus, in orders to tradesmen and in ceremonious invitations, the third person only is often used throughout: as, "*Mr. Smith will be obliged* if *Messrs. Thacker, Spink & Co.* will send *him* the books in the accompanying list; *he* would be glad to have them without delay;" or, "*Mr. J. B. Brown requests* the pleasure of *Mr. Russell Jones's* company at an Evening Party," &c. But if the writer begins by using the third person in referring to himself (instead of *I*) and in referring to the addressee (instead of *you*), the first and second persons must not subsequently be used in the letter: thus, "*Mr. Brown* presents *his* compliments to *Mr. Jones*, and hopes *you* will do *me* the favour of meeting him on the day named" is wrong.

In ordinary correspondence in English, the name of the place where the letter is written should be put near the top of the first page on the right hand side. Under it should be written the date, in the form 26*th May*, 1885, or *May* 26*th*, 1885; or the ordinal sign (*th*) may be omitted, and the date written 26 *May*, 1885.[1]

The words *Dated* and *the* before this form as, *Dated the* 26*th May*, should not be used except in strictly official correspondence.

The formula of address (*Dear Sir, &c.*) should be written somewhat lower down the page and on the left hand side.

The form of the address depends upon the amount of intimacy or the degree of relationship existing be-

---

[1] A short form, which may be used in business letters only, is 26/5/85, the /5/ standing for May, which is the fifth month in the year.

tween the writer and the person written to. The usual forms in the case of persons not relatives of the writer, are *Sir*, *Dear Sir*, *My dear Sir*, *Dear Mr. Jones*, *My dear Mr. Jones*. The first of these, *Sir*, is the most distant and formal mode of address; it is a comprehensive form, and may, with propriety, be used to high officials (unless titled) as well as to a shop-keeper. Thus, in a letter to the Lieutenant-Governor of Bengal, to a Judge of the High Court, or to the Director of Public Instruction, *Sir* is the proper form. The forms *Honoured Sir*, *Respected Sir*, though often used by Indian gentlemen in writing to official superiors, are contrary to modern English usage. There are no special terms of honour in English corresponding to the Bengali মহাশয় or আপনি. It is better that any marked honour or respect which it is desirable to show should be expressed by the general tone and style of the body of the letter, than by high-sounding titles or epithets in the address. The forms *Dear Mr. Jones* or *My dear Mr. Jones* should not be used (especially the latter), unless the writer is on terms of considerable intimacy with his correspondent.

The familiar forms *Dear Jones*, *My dear Jones* (with the *Mr.* omitted) should not be used by Indian gentlemen in addressing Europeans, unless they are on very intimate terms with them.

The forms of address for married ladies are *Madam*, *Dear Madam*, *My dear Madam*, *Dear Mrs. Jones*, *My dear Mrs. Jones*, implying different degrees of intimacy. In addressing unmarried ladies, the forms *Madam*; *Dear Madam*, *My dear Madam* would also be used, and never *Miss*, *Dear Miss*, *My dear Miss*; but when the surname is given, *Miss* should be used: as, *Dear Miss Jones, My dear Miss Jones.*

In addressing mercantile firms, *Sirs*, or *Gentlemen*, or *Dear Sirs* are the forms used, but not *Dear Gentlemen*, or *Dear Messrs. Brown & Co.*

In formal letters to *Clergymen*, instead of *Sir*, *Dear Sir*, it is proper to write *Reverend Sir*, or *Reverend and dear Sir.* But in informal letters *Dear Sir*, or *Dear Mr. Jones* are correct, even if Mr. Jones is a clergyman.

In letters to *Officers* (above the rank of Lieutenant[1]) in the army, to *Doctors* of medicine, law, &c., and to *Professors* in a University, the appropriate title should be substituted for *Mr.*: as, *Dear Colonel Smith, Dear Dr. Brown, Dear Professor Tyndall.* In more familiar letters the surname may be omitted, as *My dear Major, My dear Doctor, My dear Professor.* But in all these cases, unless considerable familiarity exists, *Sir*, or *Dear Sir*, or *My dear Sir* is used.

The correct punctuation after the address is a comma, as *Sir, My dear Mr. Smith*, and not, as is sometimes written, a note of admiration, as *Sir!*, or of interrogation, as *My dear Mr. Smith?*

The initial form of address may be repeated before the subscription; but care should be taken not to use a different form in the subscription from that used in the address; it is incorrect to begin a letter with *Dear Sir*, and end it with *I remain, Sir.*

In ordinary letters when the person addressed is not on familiar terms with the writer, it is customary to write

[1] But Lieutenants in the *Navy* are addressed by their title and not as *Mr.*

the addressee's name (as, *A. B. Jones, Esq.*) just below the writer's signature, but on the left hand side of the page. In official letters, the addressee's name is generally written at the top of the first page.[1]

In short and informal notes, especially such as are written to some one residing in the neighbourhood of the writer, the date and the name of the writer's own place of residence are often put at the end of the letter underneath and to the left of the signature. This is almost always done in letters which give or answer invitations, and in such letters the day of the week is often named (as *Friday*) in place of the date of the month, while the year is omitted (see p. 40).

The mode of ending a letter is as important as the mode of beginning it. The strictly official form of subscription is

I have the honour to be,
SIR,
Your most obedient servant,
RAM MOHAN ROY.

---

[1] In official letters from the head of an office the name and designation of the sender is written at the head of the first page followed by the official designation, if any, of the addressee or by his name if he is a non-official, as :—

(1) From
R. W. WILLIAMS, Esq.,
Magistrate and Collector.
To
The Joint Magistrate.

(2) From
A. B. SMITH, Esq.,
Secretary to the Board of Revenue.
To
Messrs. Brown, Polson & Co.

This form should be used in all business letters written to officers in their official capacity; as in letters to a Magistrate applying for an appointment, or to the Head of a College asking for admission. Another official subscription less formal than the above is

I am,
SIR,
Yours most obediently,
RAM MOHAN ROY.

This form may be fitly used in such letters as those from a student to his teacher, or from a clerk to the head of his office, asking for leave of absence.

The forms of subscription used in ordinary correspondence are *Yours faithfully*, *Yours truly*, *Yours sincerely*, which may be varied by the insertion of the adverbs *very*, *most*, *ever*, as *Yours very faithfully*, *Yours most truly*, *Yours ever sincerely*; or by changing the order of the words, as *Very faithfully yours*, *Ever most sincerely yours*.

Yours faithfully is the form expressing the least amount of familiarity, aud may be used to a perfect stranger; it is employed in ordinary business letters, where it is often contracted into *Yrs ffly*.

Yours sincerely is the form generally used between acquaintances and friends. *Yours very sincerely* implies a considerable degree of friendship. *Yours respectfully* is seldom used except by servants writing to their masters or by tradesmen writing to their customers.

It is optional whether the verb before the form of subscription (except the strictly official one) should be expressed or understood. Thus we may have *Yours truly*,

Yours most obediently, or *I remain* (or *I am*) *Yours truly* or *Believe me Yours truly.*

In letters between friends, some expression of good-will is often used to introduce gracefully the form of subscription, as *With kind regards, I am, &c., Hoping soon to hear from you, I remain, &c.*

In letters to very dear friends, the usual subscription is *Yours affectionately*, or, more simply, *Yours ever, Yours always.*

In letters to relatives, the relationship should generally be expressed: as, *Your loving brother, Your affectionate son.*

The usual form employed in directing an envelope to Englishmen is the initial letter (or letters) of the addressee's Christian name (or names), followed by the surname with the title *Esq.* (short for *Esquire*) added: as, *A. W. Smith, Esq.* The term *Esq.* is now very generally applied, being used to all except menial servants or retail traders; for the latter, the proper form of direction is *Mr.* followed by the surname, as *Mr. Smith. Messrs.* (for the French word *Messieurs*) is the usual form of direction to firms, as, *Messrs. Thacker, Spink & Co., Messrs. Smith and Sons.* Care should be taken to avoid the common error of writing *Messrs. Thacker Spink Company*, as if all three were proper names belonging to one person.

In letters directed to clergymen, the title *Rev.*, or better *The Rev.*, is used before the initials of the Christian name followed by the surname: as, *The Rev. T. S. Jones.* If the initials are not known, we may write *The Rev. Mr. Jones*, but not *The Rev. Jones.*[1]

---

[1] Similarly, *The Hon. Mr. Brown*, not *The Hon. Brown.*

There are certain other professional titles, which should always be expressed in the direction :—*The Hon.*, *The Hon'ble*, or *The Honourable*, applied to Members of Council (both supreme and provincial) or to Judges of the High Court; *General*, *Colonel*, *Major*, *Captain*, (but not *Lieutenant ;* write *Esq.*) after the name to military officers ; *Dr.*, to Doctors of medicine, law, &c.

None of these titles are applicable to the wives (as such) of those who possess the titles. Thus, do not write to the wife of a Member of Council as *The Hon'ble Mrs. Jones*, or write *Mrs. General White*, *Mrs. Doctor Brown*, &c.

The capital letters *B. A.*, *M. A.*, *M. D.*, *C.S.I.*, *&c.*, representing University Degrees[1] or titles of honour, should be placed after the name, or, if *Esq.* be used, after *Esq.* : as, *The Hon. W. Jones, C.S.I. ; The Rev. F. Wilson, M. A. ; C. R. White, Esq., B. A. ; L. W. Robinson, Esq., M. D.* When the addressee is living at the house of a third person, the letters *c/o* short for *care of* may be written before the name of the host : as

BABU HARILAL SAHA,

c/o BABU ASHUTOSH SARKAR.

The name of the post town should be written large and in a line by itself near the lower right hand edge of the envelope. The word ***at*** should never be introduced before the name of the town in directions.

---

[1] It is not the custom among Englishman to add the letters *M. A.*, *B. A.*, *&c.*, representing University Degrees, unless the letter be of a very formal character. The letters *M. D.* should not be used along with the title *Dr.*

The following are the correct forms of address and direction in the following cases :—

Person.	*Address.*	*Direction.*
King	Sir[1]	To the King's Most Excellent Majesty.
Queen	Madam[1]	To the Queen's Most Excellent Majesty.
Royal Prince	Sir[1]	To His Royal Highness The Prince of Wales.
Royal Princess	Madam[1]	To Her Royal Highness The Princess of Wales.
Archbishop	My Lord Archbishop[1]	To His Grace The Archbishop of Canterbury.
Duke	My Lord Duke[1]	To His Grace The Duke of Buckingham.
Marquis	My Lord Marquis	To the Most Noble The Marquis of Salisbury.
Earl	My Lord	To The Right Hon'ble The Earl of Leicester.
Viscount	My Lord	To the Right Hon'ble The Viscount Stradbrooke.
Baron	My Lord	To the Right Hon'ble The Lord Tennyson.
Bishop	My Lord Bishop *or* My Lord	To the Right Reverend The Lord Bishop of Ely.
Bishop (Metropolitan of India)	My Lord Bishop *or* My Lord	To the Most Reverend The Lord Bishop of Calcutta.

[1] Or, in these cases, *May it please your Majesty, May it please your Royal Highness, May it please your Grace,* may be substituted respectively.

Person.	*Address.*	*Direction.*
Other Indian Bishops	My Lord Bishop *or* My Lord	To the Right Reverend The Lord Bishop of Bombay.
Assistant Bishops	Right Reverend Sir	To the Right Reverend Bishop Clayton.
Dean	Reverend Sir	To the Reverend The Dean of St. Paul's.
Archdeacon	Reverend Sir	To the Venerable Archdeacon Browne.
Commander-in-Chief	Sir	To His Excellency The Commander-in-Chief of India.
Governor or *Lieutenant-Governor*	Sir	To the Hon'ble Sir William Hope, K.C.S.I.
Chief Justice	Sir	To the Hon'ble Sir Reginald Jones, Q. C.
Judge of the High Court	Sir	To the Hon'ble H. G. Brown.
Member of the Supreme Council	Sir	To the Hon'ble S. H. Robinson, C. S. I.
Member of a Provincial Council	Sir	To the Hon'ble D. N. Macpherson, C. I. E.
Member of the	Sir	To the Hon'ble C. H. Anderson.

In case of those who possess clerical titles or military rank in addition to other titles, the proper mode of direction will be seen from the following examples :—

To the *Reverend Sir* H. L. Jones, Bart., M.A.
To the *Honourable and Reverend* B. N. Brown, M.A.
To the *Reverend the Lord* Russell, M.A.
To *Lt.-General Sir* John Thompson.
To *General the Lord* A. Campbell.
To *Captain the Honourable* George Balfour.

The Viceroy of India should be addressed according to the rank he bears (Duke, Marquis, Earl, &c.; see above); or in place of "My Lord Duke," &c., "May it please your Excellency" may be substituted.

In the case of Royal Princes, English and Indian Noblemen, &c., any honorary titles, such as *K. G.*, *K. C. B.*, *K. T.*, *M. P.*, *K. C. S. I.*, *C. S. I.*, *C. I. E.*, should be appended to the form of Direction.

Peeresses of all the five orders are addressed as *My Lady*, and the forms of Direction are: *Her Grace the Duchess of A.*, *The Most Noble the Marchioness of B.*, *The Right Hon'ble the Countess of C.*, *The Right Hon'ble the Viscountess D.*, *The Right Hon'ble the Lady E.*

The eldest sons of Dukes, Marquises, and Earls bear some inferior title of their fathers by courtesy: thus the eldest son of the Duke of Devonshire is styled the Marquis of Hartington.

The younger sons and the daughters of Dukes and Marquises and the daughters of Earls are styled *Lords* and *Ladies*.

The younger sons of Earls and the younger sons and the daughters of Viscounts and Barons are styled *The Honourable*.

All members of Her Majesty's Privy Council are styled *The Right Hon'ble.*

Baronets, to distinguish them from Knights, have *Bart.* (short for *Baronet*) placed after their names, as *Sir Hugh Grey, Bart.* They are both addressed as *Sir.*

The *Clerical* dignity of the husband confers no title or rank upon the wife. Thus, the wife of a Bishop is not styled "My Lady," but plain "Mrs."

A few sample letters with a memorial and a petition showing the forms of address, &c., and the kind of phraseology suitable in each instance, are here given.

Chandra,
Midnapore;
21st May, 1886.

To

MESSRS. THACKER, SPINK & Co.

GENTLEMEN (*or* SIRS),

I shall be obliged if you will send me the books named in the accompanying list. I have sent a money order which will cover the price of the books and the postage.

Yours faithfully,
R—— S—— S——.

Direction on the envelope:

MESSRS. THACKER, SPINK & Co.
Publishers, &c.,
Calcutta.

136, Wellesley Street, Calcutta;
30th May, 1887.

To

THE PRINCIPAL.

SIR,

I HAVE the honour to request that you will admit me to the First Year Class from the commencement of next session.

I am,
SIR,
Your obedient servant,
U—— C—— G——

Direction on the envelope:

To

THE PRINCIPAL,
Presidency College,
Calcutta.

(*2nd Letter.*)

SIR,

I am suffering from a severe attack of fever which makes me quite unable to attend College. I beg, therefore, that you will kindly grant me leave of absence for a week.

Yours obediently,

4th April, 1885. A—— M—— C——,

2nd Year Class.

Direction on the envelope:

To

A. W. SMITH, ESQ., M. A.,

Principal,

Patna College.

To

THE INSPECTOR OF SCHOOLS,

SIR, B———.

Hearing that the post of Fourth Clerk in your office is vacant, I beg respectfully to offer myself as a candidate for the situation.

I was educated at the H—— Collegiate School and College. I passed the Entrance Examination of the —— University in the Second Division in 1882, and the First Arts Examination in the Third Division in 1884.

I have been employed for some months as an apprentice in the office of the Road Cess Engineer at H———, and have thus gained some experience in office work.

I enclose copies of testimonials as to my character and attainments.

I have the honour to be,

SIR,

Your most obedient servant,

K—— D—— M——.

13, Machooa Bazar, H———;

1st June, 1885.

Direction on the envelope:

To

THE INSPECTOR OF SCHOOLS,

B———.

To

THE CHIEF SECRETARY TO THE GOVERNMENT OF ——.

SIR,

I HAVE the honour to bring to your notice the following circumstances, and humbly to request that they may receive your kind and favourable attention.

I am a Muhammedan of the ——— family, residing in the District of N———, and my age is 18 years, 9 months.

I was educated at the N ——— Zillah School, and passed the late Entrance Examination of the University of ——— in the Third Division. I fully expected to have gained a higher place at that examination, but my illness at the time unfortunately stood in my way. To this, and to my abilities, diligence, and good character, the annexed testimonials will certify.

I am the first Muhammedan of this District that has passed the Entrance Examination, and I beg to submit that the Government has repeatedly and publicly declared its desire to encourage the Muhammedan community in the pursuit of education and in their general advancement.

I beg, therefore, respectfully to request that I may be admitted as an apprentice, without salary, into any Government Office with a view to learning the work and becoming subsequently fitted for regular employment therein, when a suitable vacancy occurs.

I have only to add that, should the opportunity be given me, I shall, by diligence and attention to my duties, do all I can to prove myself deserving of the consideration shown me.

I have the honour to be,

SIR,

Your most obedient and humble servant,

M—— A—— K——.

N————;

10th March, 188—.

To

THE MAGISTRATE AND COLLECTOR OF B——.

SIR,

I HAVE the honour respectfully to submit the following circumstances for your favourable consideration.

I am the son of respectable Hindu parents residing near B——, with whose name and benevolent deeds in the time of their prosperity you are probably not unacquainted. They have recently fallen into pecuniary difficulties, and have thus from a position of competence been suddenly reduced to poverty.

I have been for some years a pupil in the B—— Collegiate School, and had hoped to have been a candidate at the ensuing Entrance Examination of the —— University, but, in consequence of the misfortune that has befallen my family, I am now compelled to give up this hope, and must try to earn my own living.

I have received a good school education and have a fair knowledge of English, as is shown by the accompanying testimonials from the Headmaster and other masters of the Collegiate School, who also certify to my abilities, diligence, and good character.

May I, therefore, in these unfortunate circumstances, respectfully beg that you will give my case your kind consideration, and assist me as you may think best, that I may be put in the way of obtaining some employment, and so be no longer a burden but a help to my parents in their adversity.

I have the honour to be,

SIR,

Your most obedient and humble servant,

P — K— L—.

BANIPUR,

Near B——;

5th Feby. 188—.

To

THE CHIEF SECRETARY TO THE GOVERNMENT OF —.

SIR,

I HAVE the honour most respectfully to offer myself as a candidate for a post in the Subordinate Executive Service.

As regards my qualifications, I beg leave to state that I have passed the B.A. Examination of the University of——, and that

I have since devoted myself to the study of Law with some success, as the annexed testimonials will show. I have the honour also to subjoin testimonials to my moral character and fitness for Government employment from several European and Indian gentlemen. My age is 23 years, 6 months.

I am a member of a respectable D—— family, well-known and esteemed in the neighbourhood, as I believe the local Government authorities would be willing to certify; and several members of my family have served and others are still serving Government as Subordinate Judicial and Executive Officers.

I beg, therefore, humbly to submit my application for your favourable consideration, and I need hardly add that, if I should be considered deserving of an appointment, I shall do my best to perform its duties with attention and diligence.

I have the honour to be,
SIR,
Your most obedient servant,
R—— N—— C——.

D————;
3rd Novr. 188—.

To

THE DIRECTOR OF PUBLIC INSTRUCTION,——.

SIR,

I HAVE the honour humbly to lay before you the following application, praying that it may receive your favourable consideration.

I have passed the F.A. Examination of the University of—— with credit, as the accompanying testimonials will show.

I have since been employed for 3 years as third clerk in the Office of the Inspector of Schools,—— Circle, and have performed my duties to the satisfaction of my superiors, whose certificates to my efficiency are annexed. My age is 25 years.

There is not at present, and there is not likely to be for some time, any chance of my gaining promotion in the office in which I am now serving; so that, desirous as I am of obtaining some higher employment, I am compelled by circumstances to have recourse to your kindness. I do this with the sanction and approval of the Inspector, who has kindly promised to forward my application to yourself for your favourable consideration.

My object is to procure an appointment as Sub-Inspector of Schools in one of the Circles under your administration, a post for which my superiors consider me well qualified (as is shown by their testimonials), and with a view to which I have gained considerable experience in the course of my travels as clerk in attendance upon the Inspector.

May I, therefore, humbly request that you will kindly use your influence to enable me to obtain such an appointment, the duties of which I shall endeavour to perform with my best attention and diligence.

I have the honour to be,

SIR,

Your most obedient servant,

N— C— D—.

S——— ;
10th March, 188-.

To

THE CHIEF SECRETARY TO THE GOVERNMENT OF———.

SIR,

I HAVE the honour most respectfully to offer myself as a candidate for nomination by His Excellency the Viceroy and Governor-General to the Statutory Civil Service of India.

I am a member of the well-known R——— family, being a grandson of the late Rajah R——— N——— R——— and a son of Babu P——— K——— R———, who is a Deputy Magistrate and Deputy Collector in the District of N———.

I am a Master of Arts of the University of ———, having been placed in the First Class in English, in the M.A. Examination List of 188—.

I am at present engaged as Professor of English Literature in the ——— Institution. My age is 23 years, 8 months.

I beg to submit in support of my application copies of testimonials from the Hon'ble Maharajah A—— B—— C——, K.C.S.I., the Hon'ble D—— E—— F——, C.I.E., Messrs. J. B.—— and P. N——, and Pundit L—— M—— N——, C.S.I., as guarantees of my character, abilities, and fitness for the appointment for which I am a candidate.

I have the honour to be,
SIR,
Your most obedient servant,
K—— N—— R——.

59, M—— Street,
Manukabad ;
20th August, 188—.

To

THE CHIEF SECRETARY TO THE GOVERNMENT OF ——.

SIR,

I HAVE the honour to represent that I am at present serving as Deputy Magistrate and Deputy Collector of N—— in the District of D—— ; and I beg most respectfully to request the favour of my transfer from this District to that of G—— in the same Division, should such a transfer be consistent with the interests of the Public Service.

My desire for this transfer arises partly from family reasons and partly from the fact that the damp climate of this District does not suit my health, which has suffered a good deal from it for some time past.

I have the honour to submit that I have now served for seven years in this—a proverbially unhealthy—District, and that therefore my request for a transfer has some claim upon the favourable consideration of the Government.

I have the honour to be,
SIR,
Your most obedient servant,
P—— C—— N——,
Depy. Magistrate and Depy. Collector,
Aminabad.

Aminabad ;
30th May, 188—.

To

THE DIRECTOR OF PUBLIC INSTRUCTION.

SIR,

WITH the countenance and permission of the Inspector of Schools of this Circle, I have the honour to submit the following circumstances for your favourable consideration.

I am at present serving as Depûty Inspector of Schools in the District of N—— in the —— Circle, a post which I have held for the last five years.

For several months past I have suffered from repeated attacks of fever, and my medical adviser informs me that for my case change to a drier climate is absolutely necessary. His certificate to this effect is appended herewith.

I beg, therefore, respectfully to request that, subject to the interests of the Public Service, I may be transferred from my present District to any District in the —— Circle.

The Inspector of Schools of this Circle, who is acquainted with the facts of my case, has kindly consented to support my application for a transfer on the grounds stated.

I have the honour to be,

SIR,

Your most obedient servant,

C—— N—— D——.

Depy. Inspector of Schools,

N——

N——

3rd March, 188—.

To

THE PRIVATE SECRETARY TO HIS HONOUR THE LIEUTENANT-GOVERNOR OF ———.

SIR,

I BEG most respectfully to submit this my application for his Honour's favourable consideration, praying that my name may be registered as a candidate for an appointment as Deputy

Magistrate and Deputy Collector in the Subordinate Executive Service.

In support of my application, I have the honour to submit here, with copies of testimonials from ——, ——, and——, testifying to the respectability of my birth, my moral character, my general abilities, my knowledge of English, and my fitness for the appointment for which I desire to be a candidate.

I was educated at the K—— Collegiate School, and have passed the First Arts Examination of the University of——. I also studied up to the B. A. Standard of the same University, but was prevented by family circumstances from entering for the Examination. My age is 28 years.

I further venture to state that I have had some experience in different lines of work in the Public Service, having held an acting appointment as Head Clerk in the office of the Commissioner of the B—— Division, and having also for a short time served as Inspector of Post Offices in the Districts of M—— and N——. I am at present a Junior Clerk in the office of the Accountant-General of B——.

I have for the past five years devoted much of my time to the study of English literature and to reading English books, and I have also had the opportunity of mixing, to some extent, in European society, to the improvement of my mental culture and knowledge of affairs.

Should his Honour be pleased to grant my application, I shall do my best to perform diligently and conscientiously the duties of the post to which I may be appointed.

I have the honour to be,

SIR,

Your most obedient servant,

A—— B—— C——.

10, Nuddea Street,
KULITULAH;
25th February, 188—.

To

THE CHIEF SECRETARY TO THE GOVERNMENT OF——.

The Humble Memorial of A—— M—— C——

Respectfully sheweth :

That your Memorialist is a graduate (M. A. 188— and B. L. 188—) of the University of ——, and that during the whole of his Collegiate career he held a first grade Government Scholarship and obtained the —— College Undergraduates' Gold Medal in 188— and a Silver Medal for proficiency in English, together with several College Prizes.

2. That your Memorialist, upon taking his B. L. degree, was employed for two years as Law Lecturer in the —— College, after which period he served for three years as Head Clerk in the Registry Office, N——. Finding, however, that there was no prospect of promotion in that department of the Government Service, he resigned his situation in order to qualify himself for higher employment by joining the legal profession. He is at present a Pleader of more than two years' standing in the High Court of N——.

3. That your Memorialist belongs to a respectable Hindu family, well known in the time of its prosperity for its works of charity and benevolence; and the petitioner's father, the late Babu C—— M—— G—— was a faithful servant of Government for twenty years in the Subordinate Executive Service.

4. That your Memorialist has always himself been desirous of entering the same service, but that when the rules for admission into that service by open competition were published, he had passed the prescribed age limit of 25 years by only 16 days, and was consequently just excluded from entering for the examination, which your petitioner believes he was fully qualified to pass. He is now 27 years of age.

5. Your Memorialist, therefore, humbly prays that, under the circumstances, he may either be permitted to compete at the next Examination for admission into the Subordinate Executive Service, or that the Government may be graciously pleased to appoint him to that service by Nomination.

6. Your Memorialist has the honour to submit herewith printed copies of testimonials in his favour, certifying to his moral character, abilities, and general fitness for employment in the above mentioned service.

And your Memorialist, as in duty bound, will ever pray.

11, Mitter's Lane,
RAMANIPUR ;
The 19th December, 188—.

To

HIS HONOUR THE LIEUTENANT-GOVERNOR OF———.

The Humble Petition of M——— R——.

Respectfully sheweth :

That your Petitioner is a member of the R——— family residing in the district of N———, where it is well-known for its works of benevolence and charity. His age is 23 years, 10 months.

2. That your Petitioner was educated at the N——— College, from which he passed the First Arts Examination of the ——University in 187—, and that in 188— he passed the higher grade Pleadership Examination. Copies of his certificates are appended herewith.

3. That your Petitioner has since been practising as Pleader in the local Courts with fair success. He has always taken a warm interest in local affairs, and has, he believes, succeeded in winning the esteem of the people and the officials of the District in which he resides.

4. Wherefore your Petitioner humbly prays that your Honour will be graciously pleased to give his case your favourable consideration, so that he may be appointed to some post in the Subordinate Executive Service either in this or in another district under your Honour's administration, the duties of which post it shall always be his best endeavour to perform with diligence and fidelity.

And your Petitioner, as in duty bound, will ever pray.

BARIPUR ;
The 10th May, 188—.

Testimonials.—In drawing up Testimonials to the character or abilities of another, be careful to avoid all exaggeration. Remember that excessive eulogy defeats its own object, and is likely to do the applicant harm rather than good. Let your language be plain, straightforward, and to the point. Mention all you know to his credit, and no more; and state your opinion as to his abilities moderately and concisely. Do not wander off into vague generalities; if you cannot conscientiously commend the person of whom you write, it is best to excuse yourself from giving him any Testimonial at all.

In writing a Testimonial, introduce first the full name and title (if any) of the applicant, and mention the period during which you have known him, together with a brief statement of his creditable performances hitherto. Then give your own opinion as to his merits and abilities, and close (if you will) with a polite wish for his success.

In signing your name at the end of a Testimonial, be careful to append any Degree or title you may possess (as, M. A., C. S. I., &c.) and add your designation (as, *Deputy Magistrate and Deputy Collector, &c.*). This is done in the interests of the applicant, since the higher your position, the more weight is attached to your statements.

A few examples are appended.

BABU M——— A———M——— has asked me for a Testimonial. He has served under me as junior clerk in the office of the Director of Public Instruction, ———, for about a year, and has done his work well. He is punctual, industrious, and obliging, and I have much pleasure in recommending him for promotion to a higher appointment. He has my best wishes for his success.

M———;
June 3rd, 188—.

D—— N—— G——, B.A.,
Head Clerk,
Office of the Director of Public Instruction,
M———.

I beg to state that I have known Babu N——— M——— N——— for a considerable time, and that I have a high opinion of his moral worth. He is a young man of good birth and gentlemanly manners and address. He possesses excellent abilities and business-like habits, combined with much tact and discretion. He has my best wishes for the success of his present application.

G———;
3rd November, 188—.

S—— N—— C——, B.A.,
Sub.-Depy. Collector,
G———.

I have been acquainted with Babu R——— N——— D——— for the last three years, and have every reason to believe that his moral character is excellent. He has a high reputation in this district for his abilities, energy, and perseverance in the discharge of his duties. He comes of a good family, and is courteous and affable in his bearing.

K—— L—— B——, M.A.,
Deputy Inspector of Schools,
R———.

R———;
3rd August, 188—.

Certified that Moulvie M——— A——— belongs to a respectable family, that he bears a good character, and possesses fair abilities. He is, in my opinion, well fitted for Government employment in a subordinate capacity.

S—— A—— N——, M.A.,
Dy. Magistrate & Dy. Collector,
B———.

B———;
August 20th, 188—.

I have much pleasure in certifying that I have known Babu N—— M—— M——, B.L., for the past five years. I also know his father very intimately, who is a Government pensioner, and holds a highly respectable position in the Indian community. His son possesses good abilities and an excellent character, and is, in my opinion, well qualified to discharge efficiently the duties of an *employé* in the Subordinate Executive Service.

R—— M—— G——,
Barrister of the High Court,
L——.

BAR LIBRARY;
January 5th, 188—.

BABU M—— C—— S——, B.A., has asked me for a Testimonial. I have been acquainted with him for the last five years, and have seen or heard of him from time to time. In 187— he obtained the B. A. degree, in the 1st class, in the University of ——. He has since discharged the duties of Headmaster of the N—— Middle Class English School, with energy and success. I believe him to be a young man of good character and abilities, and likely to do good work in the post for which he is making application.

D—— N—— B——,
Deputy Inspector of Schools,
N——.

N——;
3rd May, 188—.

I have known Babu R—— C—— D—— for a considerable time. For the past three years he has been serving as clerk (class I) in the office of the Accountant-General of B——, where I have had many opportunities of testing his abilities. He is a good and intelligent worker, is diligent in and attentive to his duties, and knows English well. He is very respectably connected, and his character and behaviour have always been excellent. I regard him as well fitted for higher employment under Government.

R—— C—— M——, B.L., C.I.E.,
Assistant Accountant-General,
B——.

The Treasury;
10th March, 188—.

BABU F—— K—— B——, B.A., joined this College after passing the Entrance Examination and read for the B. A. Examination which he passed in 188—. I have, therefore, had sufficient opportunity of judging of his work and abilities; and I consider him to be a young man with a good head, much perseverance, and steady habits. His behaviour in College has always been excellent, and, as far as I am aware, his moral character is all that can be desired. I have no hesitation in recommending him for suitable employment under Government or elsewhere.

B—— M—— K——, M.A.,
Professor of Mathematics,
C—— College.

C——;
7th May, 188—.

I beg to certify that Moonshi A—— R—— officiated for three months as Mohrir in the Road Cess Office, P——, and that he did his work well. He has a fair knowledge of English and bears a good character.

A—— A —— K——,
Deputy Collector.

P—— Collectorate;
5th December, 188—.

I have much pleasure in giving a testimonial in favour of Moulvie A—— A—— K——. He belongs to one of the most respectable Muhammedan families in P——. He is well educated and well-mannered, and I know nothing against his moral character. I have been acquainted with him and with his family for a long period, and I can unhesitatingly testify to his intellectual abilities and to his habits of diligence and attention to business, which would, I believe, well fit him for a post in the Government Service.

S—— D—— R——, C.S.I.,
Zemindar of N——.

P——;
12th April, 188—.

Addresses.—In composing Addresses for presentation to European gentlemen in their public capacity or to public bodies, be chary of exaggerated expressions of esteem or of a profusion of compliment. An excessive display of sentiment in compositions of this kind, sounds strained and unreal to English ears; do not, therefore, give too much indulgence to the softer emotions, but leave them for the most part to be understood. If, for instance, you and your friends wish to express your grief at the retirement of the gentleman who is the subject of the Address, do so gravely and soberly, and do not say that your heart is breaking or that your eyes swim with tears at the thought of his leaving you. An enumeration of the good or kind deeds, moderately worded, of the person so addressed, may often fitly form part of such a composition, accompanied by an expression of gratitude for their bestowal and of sorrow at his departure, the whole closing with hopes and good wishes for his future welfare and happiness.

INDEX